Bright Lights, Dark Shadows

The Shadow Side of Celebrity and Fame

Mimi Amaral

Crescendo
PUBLISHING

Bright Lights, Dark Shadows: The Shadow Side of Celebrity and Fame
By Mimi Amaral

Crescendo Publishing, LLC
2-558 Upper Gage Ave., Ste. 246
Hamilton, ON L8V 4J6
Canada

GetPublished@CrescendoPublishing.com
1-877-575-8814

ISBN: 978-1-948719-06-3 (p)
ISBN: 978-1-948719-07-0 (e)

Printed in the United States of America
Cover design by Gracia Chacón

10 9 8 7 6 5 4 3 2 1

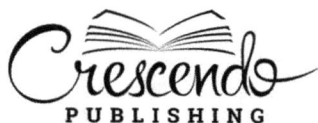
PUBLISHING

Message from the Author

First, acknowledgement and gratitude to Source/ Cosmos (AKA: God). Without divine guidance, none of this would have manifested.

I will never say I have the answers, because I do not. All I can say is that I can hold a safe space to toss ideas around so a co-creation of answers may be manifested. Within this book, I have spoken about shadow aspects in order to bring them to the surface to be seen, acknowledged, and integrated into the collective and individual consciousness. By bringing the unconscious "Shadow" Truths into the light, maybe a co-creation of preventative wellness may begin to manifest. Also, within this book, I have not just complained and brought shadow forth; I've asked pertinent questions and made suggestions for improvement.

I hope this book allows for a different perspective of the world of entertainment and sports to be brought forth, allowing all to embody celebrity and fame from the entertainers' and athletes' subjective reality.

Endorsements

"As a psychologist with thirty years of experience working with and writing about musicians and other artists' mental health concerns, I support the creation of an Entertainment Division in the APA. Division 10, the APA Arts Division, has not traditionally addressed clinical issues pertaining to performers despite the profound impact the psychology of these artists continues to have on the culture as a whole. Other organizations, such as the Performing Arts Medicine Association (PAMA), have provided much-needed attention to the health and special needs of performers, but psychology continues to be a minor focus relative to physical medicine.

Considering the enormous wealth surrounding the entertainment industry, one might hope that an APA Division of Entertainment could help legitimize increased funding for scientific study, which has been sorely lacking to date. Areas of potential interest that I would like to see addressed within this new Division include such topics as: occupational stress and coping processes over the career life span (including similarities and differences amongst artistic professions and subgenres); the dynamics between performer health and development and the corporate interests and demands of the entertainment industry; the influence of cultural portrayals of artists on artists themselves and the Public, particularly adolescents, and the breakdown of such stereotypes."

— Susan D. Raeburn, Ph.D.

"I support the new APA Division 'Entertainment Psychology.' I'm a musician, and I've had a professional career in the music industry as a lead vocalist for several signed bands in Europe and the U.S., which included the release of several albums and music videos as well as promoting our music on tour. After 15 years in the recording studio and on the road playing shows, I decided to go back to school in order to become a psychologist. I've been in private practice for a few years now and I'm excited to see 'Entertainment Psychology' emerge as a new division of the APA. I believe there is a tremendous need for psychologists in the entertainment industry in order to provide education, therapy, crisis intervention, and psychological testing. In addition, I support psychologists conducting research and contributing to prevention and early intervention specifically tailored to artists, staff, and executives in the entertainment industry."

— Ralph G. Kuechle, Ph.D.,
Clinical Psychologist

"I support the new APA Division 'Entertainment Psychology.' I have been peripherally associated with the entertainment industry through my participation as a semi-professional musician as well as having friends in the television news industry. I see a need for mental health support for those in the entertainment industry in order to support the creative process and to assist in dealing with creative differences, burnout, adapting to celebrity, and the ability to work productively in a group without the intrusion of maladaptive familial communication patterns that can make creative work more complicated. I am not

aware of any current programs that exist to facilitate the maintenance of mental health for those in the entertainment business, as evidenced by the frequent reports of 'meltdowns' and other tragic consequences related to the immense pressures of this business (e.g., substance abuse, family break ups, difficult adult adjustment for child actors, etc.). I can also see the utility of supporting the smooth completion of projects as being attractive to those who manage entertainment projects and other entities that are responsible for assuring the completion of these projects. I will soon be completing my doctoral education in psychology and would be interested in joining the APA and the Entertainment Psychology division in order to support the provision of education, therapy, crisis intervention, and psychological testing. Psychologists conducting research and contributing to prevention and early intervention specifically tailored to artists, staff, and executives in the entertainment industry can only be seen as beneficial and long overdue."

— Michael Murray, LMFT,
Marriage and Family Therapist,
Psy-D Candidate

"I'm surprised a specialized psychology division for the entertainment industry has not been developed yet, especially with all the tragedies over the years and the difficulty entertainers have transitioning out of childhood roles into adulthood.

I support the idea of Entertainment Psychology because I have had a firsthand view that success is a killer, rejection is a killer, and the combination of the two are lethal. Once one has a taste of success, any rejection begins to erode one's being, creating stress, uncertainty, and self doubt (i.e. I'm not good enough, I'm too old, I'm not pretty enough, I'm too heavy). Additionally, in the early days of Hollywood, one was protected by the studio system; now, however, one is left to fend for themselves. Any move made by an entertainer is subject to exploitation, magnification, and judgment in the media and by society.

Furthermore, fame and/or loss of fame also affects family, friends, fans, and people surrounding the entertainer. People identify with an entertainer in a subjective way, whether the person knows the entertainer personally or not; hence stalkers. That said, even the people close to the entertainer may become someone else during the height of the entertainer's fame and success, and then the relationships can transition toward darkness and dissolve when the entertainer is no longer capturing the spotlight.

I believe everyone wants mental and physical health. I also believe a specialized focus in an industry like this one would help not only entertainers who are in the business but help guide young adults who are trying so hard to become the next Elizabeth Taylor or Robert Redford."

— Ken Davitian,
Actor/Producer

Table of Contents

Dedication 1

Foreword 3

Chapter 1: Lifestyle Risks 9

Chapter 2: Lack of Personal Space...........................33

Chapter 3: Fall from Grace.......................................55

Chapter 4: Observation and Integration..................77

Chapter 5: Shadow to Light......................................91

About the Author 111

About Entertainment Psychology 113

Other Books by Mimi Amaral 115

Connect with the Author...117

Acknowledgements..119

References..121

Dedication

To all the entertainers and athletes who feel they are alone with no witness. May this book help bring awareness to the shadow side of the industry so we may co-create a healthy environment to live within.

Please support the movement for preventative measure for celebrity mental health and wellness by signing the petition for an APA Entertainment Psychology division at:

apa.org/about/division/formation-petitions.aspx

Foreword

By Dr. Tami Gager, Ed.D.,
Developmental Psychologist and Professor

Carl Jung introduced the concepts of archetypes, the collective unconscious, and the shadow to modern psychodynamic theory. Building and expanding on the work of Freud, he first introduced the concept of archetypes and collective unconscious in 1916. Later in his career, Jung expanded on his idea of archetypes to include the shadow in 1938. Since he first introduced these ideas, they have become mainstays in modern psychology. In Jungian psychology, the shadow refers to unconscious aspects of our personalities, of which we may not ever be aware. Jung stated that the shadow is, in essence, our dark side.

Because humans have a tendency to remain unaware or ignorant of their least desirable personality traits, the shadow is comprised mostly of those negative attributes. There are also positive aspects that may remain hidden in a person's shadow. This is especially true of people with low self-esteem, negative self-image, anxiety, depression, or false beliefs about themselves. Each person has a shadow side. According to Jung, the less the shadow is apparent in a person's conscious life, the blacker and deeper it is. Meaning, the more hidden or subconscious the shadow, the darker it is.

Even before Jung's work on the shadow was his work on the collective unconscious. The collective unconscious is different from our individual, personal unconscious in that it is shared across human beings. We all have our own personal unconscious that contains our drives and our moral and ethical compass. Nevertheless, the drives and moral compass that all human beings have originate from the human collective—the set of beliefs and symbols that we share, yet cannot necessarily pinpoint their origin. Jung stated the collective unconscious was essentially the soul of humanity. As a group, the human collective unconscious is occupied by instincts and archetypes, including universal symbols like our shadow.

In American society, the collective unconscious contains its own shadow. The collective unconscious we Americans share has allowed us to liberate ourselves from oppressive government, advance technologically, lead the world through ideas and action, become an economic superpower, and be outspoken on human rights. These are the attributes America shows, the presenting self of our nation; however, American society also has a shadow. Arrogance, sociocentrism, entitlement, and hubris have all been used to describe the shadow side of America.

Another aspect of the American shadow is our treatment of celebrities. There is a collective belief that celebrities and entertainers should live their lives under public scrutiny and be grateful to do so because it is simply the price of fame. We want our celebrities to speak up for causes, to be present and "on" for us in public, to respond to us via social media, and to embody the charisma and characters they portray in film, on stage, or on the playing field. The truth of the shadow is that Americans want our celebrities to speak up for the causes—but only our personal causes.

If we do not share the same belief, we tell them that they are celebrities and should keep their opinions to themselves. If our celebrities do not fully engage in public, take interviews, or submit to the paparazzi, we call them ingrates and say they need to be humbler. If our celebrities gain weight or have a fashion misstep, we ridicule them for not meeting our ideal image. Often, these conflicting ideas of celebrity and the shadow of celebrity cause a number of problems. Drug abuse and addiction, loneliness, isolation, anxiety, depression, and self-harm and suicide can all be the effects of the American shadow on celebrities.

The author of this book, Dr. Mimi Amaral, wishes to shed light on multiple aspects of the shadow side of celebrity. Mimi has worked to promote a new category of psychology, Entertainment Psychology, in the hopes of creating a field very much like Sports Psychology. Mimi's interest in Entertainment Psychology came in the form of an intangible message from the Universe. She was walking to her car one night and heard a loud voice from the Universe tell her she had to develop Entertainment Psychology. Grateful to be alone, she spoke to herself and said, "That is an interesting idea." The next day she called the American Psychological Association (APA) to inquire if such a field already existed. She was told that fields are known as divisions at the APA, and this division did not yet exist. During that phone call, Mimi also learned that one must be a doctor to start the petition process. Mimi never wanted to be a doctor; it was not anywhere in her life's aspirations. Her next steps were to attend a doctoral program and conduct research on the topic. With the support of a professor she respected greatly, Mimi developed the concept for her dissertation, which was ultimately adapted into this book.

Mimi's goal in creating this unique division of psychology is that it will ultimately lead to training psychologists to specialize in treating the unique mental health problems and psychosocial stressors that arise from fame, and create counseling platforms to teach celebrities coping skills for the many shadow aspects that arise from their fame. This book illuminates the shadow side of fame and illustrates how many of the stories of celebrity bad behavior, mental illness, and suicide are related to the American shadow and society's collective unconscious.

"To go in the dark with a light is to know the light. To know the dark, go dark. Go without sight, and find that the dark, too, blooms and sings, and is traveled by dark feet and dark wings."

~ Wendell Berry

Chapter 1

Lifestyle Risks

*"It is strange to be known so universally
and yet to be so lonely."*

~ Albert Einstein

Loneliness and Isolation

There are a number of shadow aspects that celebrities encounter with their celebrity status, such as feelings of loneliness and isolation. Loneliness specifically has long been a complaint among celebrities. Giles states, "Loneliness has been described as the *feeling* of isolation, as opposed to isolation itself, and this can often be caused by the absence of a confidant, or of a 'reliable alliance'—someone to be trusted in times of anxiety." Furthermore, loneliness leads to multiple undesirable issues and life complications. Tatlilioglu explains in his writing that loneliness leads to the development of problems in the individual by making the individual have emotional difficulty. Among these problems are anger directed toward self and others, depression, self-pity and social disharmony, shyness, low life satisfaction and sadness, sleep and anxiety disorder, hopelessness, thought of and attempted suicide, low optimism and subjective well-being, interpersonal and eating disorders, cognitive distortions, avoidance of affiliation and nonfunctional attitudes, thoughts of death and withdrawal from social interaction, and social harmony difficulty.

An example of loneliness and isolation is observable in Charlie Chaplin's autobiography. Chaplin described, in detail, the negative emotions induced by all the attention he received—not only from fans, but also family and friends who began excessively crowding in on him. Chaplin was perplexed by the actions of people once he achieved fame. He expressed that he wanted to enjoy it all without reservation, but felt instead as if the world had gone insane. Chaplin stated, "If a few slapstick comedies could arouse such excitement, was there not something bogus about all celebrity?" Chaplin had always thought he would like the public's attention; however, he realized that it paradoxically isolated him with a depressing sense of loneliness.

Tending to so many people and encountering the loss of privacy would be unfathomable for anyone who has not achieved stardom. Throughout history, fame and celebrity has been portrayed as glitz and glamour with a chance to evade predominate life stressors. Braudy describes, "The dream of fame in Western society has been inseparable from the ideal of personal freedom. In search of modern fame we often enter a world of obvious fiction, in which all blemishes are smoothed and all wounds healed. "Whereas Evans and Wilson discuss how fame is actually more of a conundrum:

"It is a great paradox that many people seek fame and wealth in order to gain freedom from the demands of others, only to discover a new set of pressures and constraints. "The ideal image of fame and celebrity has always been acknowledged, while the problematic areas have been banished into the shadow. From the shadow perspective, Johnson explains that, "We are presently dealing with the accumulation of a whole society that has worshipped its light side and refused the dark..."

Like a commodity, celebrities are often required to perform or be social and engage with fans, the media, and entertainment industry professionals—regardless of how they may feel personally. From the moment entertainers and athletes reach celebrity status, they are expected to relinquish their privacy and personal space. With global recognition and expectations, it would be understandable to experience isolation and loneliness. Throughout the literature on the shadow, it is indicated that where there is light there must be equal amounts of dark. Johnson, who writes on the shadow of the unconscious (unintegrated unconscious conditioning/beliefs), exemplifies the harmonizing of light and shadow through a seesaw metaphor. Johnson uses the seesaw metaphor to explain that we must be balanced if one is to remain in equilibrium; if one indulges characteristics on the right side, they must be balanced by an equal weight on the left side. Therefore, the celebrity factor of recognition and notoriety can be countered by isolation and loneliness. It is problematic to think one exists without the other. However, it is common for people to shun and/or repress the undesirable aspects into the shadow (unconscious).

To further depict the loneliness and isolation of fame and celebrity, Dr. Donna Rockwell and Dr. David Giles state in their research that, "Immediately upon entering the sphere of fame, relationships to 'self' and 'others' are profoundly affected. The public wants a piece of them, to touch them, to get an autograph, to have their picture taken with the star. All the while, hearing one's name screamed out, the famous person feels as if he or she is not even there. Participants find themselves at a loss when members of the public can 'hardly contain themselves' at the sight of them and 'make you larger than life.' "It is lonely for persons who find themselves alone and isolated on an island of recognition, where "there's a loneliness that happens because you are separate."

It may be assumed that with so many people surrounding entertainers and athletes, and with the attention they receive daily, loneliness would be impossible. However, if a person is not being seen for whom they truly are, and only being recognized for what has been falsely manufactured through a persona and their work, then loneliness can be conceivable. The concept of a romantic relationship is a good metaphor. In some relationships, individuals might complain that their partner does not even know or see them for who they are, even though they live together in the same house. This metaphor can also be applied to entertainers or athletes.

People tend to project their own subjective reality and expectations onto the celebrity without knowing anything about the person behind the public image. Crain speaks on Jung's theory of the shadow. In his writing, he explains the consequences that occur when only one part of person is valued. Crain stipulates that Jung believed the persona, or public image, is important to achieve one's goals in society; however, the persona should not be developed in a one-sided way. When this happens, the individual becomes an empty shell. The individual needs to develop a balance between the persona and the deeper aspects of his or her personality.

The exposure society receives of entertainers and athletes from viewing television or reading magazines is not an accurate portrayal of the person. On occasion, however, entertainers and athletes may reveal the authentic self behind the persona. Society, if they pay close attention, can get a glimpse of the person.

A good example was during the Golden Globe Awards in January of 2013.Jodie Foster accepted her award while talking about her career, her former partner, and her loneliness. At the end of her speech she stated, "I want to be seen, to be understood deeply, and to be not so very lonely. "In addition, Beal states that women can be more susceptible to loneliness: "Women may be more vulnerable to loneliness because they live longer and experience events such as the death of spouses and relocation with great frequency." One result of these changes and losses may be the disruption of women's social network. The innate implication of fame and celebrity considerably inhibit building trusted and dependable social networks for men and women, which can contribute to the feeling of loneliness and isolation.

As stated by prominent sports psychologist Dr. Steve Peters, "Some athletes get the feeling that the whole world is against them, especially when the media might be involved too. "Peters notes, "They can feel that what is being written about them is unfair but is what people will believe. This may have a knock-on effect which can decrease self-esteem and create further feelings of being alone."

Professional football (soccer) player Thomas Hitzlsperger stated, "Toward the end of my career I got that loneliness feeling. There were times when I wanted to talk with someone but I couldn't. Of course I am not talking to my teammates, we talk about football, we don't talk about private matters." Additionally, Paula Ratcliffe, marathon world record holder in 2003, reported that, "After Athens was a difficult time for me because then it was knowing who you could talk to. That is who your best friends are, and whom you can open up to. You need to know they are not going to go to the media or abuse that trust of being able to share your inner thoughts, inner concerns, and inner worries with them."

Other celebrities who encountered loneliness were Health Ledger and Michael Jackson. The biography of Health Ledger discloses, "As his anxiety increased, his loneliness overwhelmed him and, as the long, dark New York night wore on, Heath seems to have fallen back on his prescription medications to help him relax." Michael Jackson on many occasions spoke about his loneliness. He stated, "Success definitely brings on loneliness. People think that you are lucky, that you have everything. They think you can go anywhere and do anything, but that's not the point. One hungers for the basic stuff...People think they know me, but they don't, not really. Actually, I am one of the loneliest people on this earth. I cry sometimes because it hurts.

It does. To be honest, I guess you could say that it hurts to be me."

Additionally, during a VH1 interview in 1996, Michael Jackson discussed the highs and lows of fame—singing about the pitfalls on his track "Stanger in Moscow," which was later explained to be entirely autobiographical. The song has themes of loneliness and isolation, including lyrics like "Here abandoned in my fame/Armageddon of the brain."

Anxiety, Depression, and Meltdowns

There are additional afflictions co-existing with celebrity and fame, including anxiety, depression, and meltdowns. Ludwig argues, "Fame is not all fun and games, however; the cost of fame can be high. For example, the frequency of mental disorders runs as high as seventy-three percent in artists and sixty-eight in musicians. "The prevalence of anxiety and depression discussed in the research by Bjerkeset, Nordahl, Larsson, Dahl, and Linaker highlights that anxiety and depression are common in the public. It is accepted by most psychologists and psychotherapists that symptom overlap between anxiety and depression is the rule rather than the exception. This further contributes to the individual's impairment and symptom burden compared to depression or anxiety alone. Bjerkeset and colleagues argue that both anxiety and depression exist within the general populous, which would not exclude the entertainment industry. Moreover, it has been documented that entertainers often suffer from these disorders throughout their careers.

Entertainers and athletes are not exempt from anxiety. In fact, many have reported trouble with anxiety, panic attacks, and social anxiety disorders. Entertainers who have openly discussed their encounters with anxiety include George Michael, Donny Osmond, LeAnn Rimes, Adele, Nicole Kidman, Barbra Streisand, Naomi Judd, Roseanne Barr, and Kim Basinger. The prevalence of anxiety disorders among entertainers can be indicative of continuously being in the public eye. Danity states that it can be emotionally and mentally draining for those living the celebrity lifestyle, in the spotlight, and being examined daily by society. Heath Ledger was also one who suffered from anxiety and depression. Rob writes, "Ledger was never particularly good at being alone: on his own he could be overwhelmed by self-pity, depression and his anxiety about his career, his abilities and the paranoia that he was being stalked by aggressive paparazzi." Another artist who discussed experiencing high anxiety was George Michael. He reported to ABC News that his anxiety could become debilitating at times. Michael said, "Although I was right to believe that the shows would bring me great happiness and that my voice would recover completely, I was wrong to think I could work my way through the major anxiety that has plagued me since I left Austria last December."

Research completed by psychologist Jonathan Abramowitz, of the University of North Carolina, told *ABC News* that nearly one in four people suffer from clinical anxiety disorders, including panic attacks. Some are genetically disposed, and other times it may occur due to an incident. When it begins to interfere with a person's performance, causes a great deal of distress, or is painful to the point of trouble sleeping, then it crosses the line into a clinical problem.

In Donny Osmond's autobiography, he revealed his doctor assessed him and discovered he had social phobia. Osmond disclosed that he would break into a sweat and experience panic before he took the stage to perform. Additionally, singer-songwriter LeAnn Rimes voluntarily admitted herself into a mental health facility in August of 2012. ABC News reported that Rimes said, "This is just a time for me to emotionally check out for a second and take care of myself and come back in thirty days as the best 30-year-old woman I can be. All the things in life will be there when I get out, but you know what? I'm hoping they're not going to affect me as much."

The previous statements are exemplar of the human factor being eradicated and tossed into the shadow of the industry. The effects are not eliminated because the problem is rarely discussed. In fact, it can be argued that the lack of discussion only exacerbates the consequences and outcomes. Entertainers are just people, and like anyone else, pushing them as products or machines can create a breaking point, resulting in a meltdown.

The most publicized meltdowns may have been Britney Spears and Lindsey Lohan. Stevens of *New York Magazine* reported on Spears' meltdown: "I caught up with the divorce and the party binge, the pantyless [sic] paparazzi photos, and the vomiting on her entourage. After the hair came off, she'd gone to a tattoo parlor and, weeping and screaming, inked a kiss on her wrist and a cross on her hip. The next day she was wearing a cheap 'Marilyn' wig. Unlike Madonna, Spears' has never called her own shots. She is just a money-making toy adults sell children. The press rarely calls her 'Spears.' That might suggest she's human. She's Britney, the singing Barbie. A concoction. She was first marketed as a child celebrity—beginning as a Mouseketeer—and then, when she filled out, transformed into teen cheese. Her mortification of the flesh at 25 is just the latest example of how bizarrely troubling American society finds the female body. The sacrificial standard was, of course, set by Marilyn Monroe. It made perfect sense for Spears, after her mortification, to hide as Marilyn."

Another artist who was conflicted was Lindsay Lohan. There have been a number of highly publicized events, including Lohan's meltdown during a rehab stint for Adderall abuse. In 2013, it was reported by *INQUISITR* that Lohan had apparently reached rock bottom during her time at the Betty Ford Center, after being denied Adderall during her 90-day court required treatment. When Lohan was denied her Adderall, the young celebrity reportedly took a turn for the worse; her friends and family were afraid that Lohan might run away from rehab at any time. Apparently, the situation had gotten so bad that "the actor look[ed] extremely haggard, her face [was] bloated, and it [did not appear] she had brushed her hair in days. She look[ed] very disheveled and had absolutely no energy after the doctors took away her Adderall."

It seems that there have been many entertainers who have experienced meltdowns. *Us Weekly* alone has reported on the following entertainers who have suffered public meltdowns: Mel Gibson, Amanda Bynes, and Nick Stahl. One report in 2013 disclosed that Gibson was caught on tape commenting to Joe Eszterhas, screenwriter of *Maccabees,* "Why don't I have a first draft of *The Maccabees?* What the fuck have you been doing?" Gibson could be heard screaming at Eszterhas on the recording. Eszterhas and Gibson were working together on the *Maccabees* film, but Eszterhas claimed Gibson never intended to make it because "he hates Jews. "Gibson also sounded off on the recording about his ex-girlfriend, Oksana Grigorieva, screaming, "I am earning money to a filthy little cocksucker who takes advantage of me!" Eszterhas stated, "The bottom line is it shows to me he badly needs help."

Us Weekly also reported that actress Amanda Bynes (*The Amanda Show, Rugrats, What a Girl Wants*) had a meltdown and, after displaying some erratic behavior and setting fire on the driveway of a stranger, was put on a Section 5150 of the California Welfare and Institutions Code psychiatric hold as a danger to herself and others. Additionally, actor Nick Stahl (*Terminator 3, Carnivàle, Sin City*) was also placed on a 5150 psychiatric hold following an undisclosed incident.

Us Weekly has not been the only outlet reporting on the shadow of the industry. *People* magazine reported on Mischa Barton's breakdown in 2013: "Strapped to a gurney at Cedars-Sinai medical Center, Mischa Barton threatened to kill herself. It was July 15, 2009, and the 23-year-old—who had rocketed to fame as the star of the FOX series *The O.C.*—was frightened and frantic. A few hours earlier, Barton had been confronted by her parents and agents at her home in Los Angeles; she was under massive stress, working nonstop and partying even harder. Scared by her increasingly erratic behavior and worried she was in no condition to fly to New York for a scheduled appearance the next week, those closest to her staged an intervention. The young actor felt the walls closing in, and she had taken a powerful sedative to combat anxiety. Not long after the meeting, Barton blacked out and was rushed to the hospital; there, she became more distraught and was restrained by staff after she fought them and tried to leave. In the frenzy, Barton threatened suicide."

As for athletes, reported by *The Telegraph*, Olympic star Victoria Pendleton disclosed causing self-harm due to the demands of the elite sports. Pendleton confessed to *The Telegraph* reporter that, "From the age of 15 she suffered anxiety and self-loathing. Success didn't help. The first time she cut herself was after making the British cycling squad. She couldn't understand why she felt so insecure. 'I was not starving; I was not in a war zone. I was a white middle-class, 23-year-old girl from the Home Counties. I was in the midst of an opportunity of a lifetime. What right did I have to feel so bereft?"

Other athletes have suffered from anxiety and psychological disorders. As reported by the OCD Center of Los Angeles, the following athletes have struggled: Ricky Williams (Miami Dolphins) has long struggled with social anxiety; Earl Campbell (Hall of Fame running back) struggled with panic disorder; David Beckham (LA Galaxy, Manchester United) openly discussed having obsessive compulsive disorder; and Clint Malarchuk (NHL, IHL) has also openly discussed having obsessive compulsive disorder.

Trying to meet expectations of a public image while suppressing aspects that are innate within the entertainer or athlete will only create dissonance. The previously mentioned public meltdowns are vivid examples of repressed energy manifesting in many celebrities and athletes. For many celebrities, there will eventually come a breaking point—and not only could harm come to one's self, but there is a possibility that harm may also come to others. Keeping emotions, thoughts, wants, and needs pushed down within will only create a volcanic effect that is bound to erupt in one way or another at some point.

As discussed, a person's shadow is anything that is not integrated into their conscious life. The rigidity of the bright lights of fame, without being able to express the dark side of celebrity and fame, is a prime example of Jung's theory of shadow. Through the shadow lens, it is also understood that the archetype can be universal and developed within a cultural context as well. Naturally, cultural contexts consisting of values, beliefs, and languages of a group would exist. It could even be argued that celebrity has its own culture. Zweig, in his research, explains: "Cultural differences in relation to competition and winning, for example, yield different shadow content: Dutch children, who need to be prepared to live in an egalitarian society, are taught that coming in first is not necessarily a virtue; they learn to keep low profiles, thereby banishing their ambition into the shadow."

Zweig's example mirrors celebrity culture by highlighting the attributes of celebrity and fame, while exiling the problematic aspects such as loneliness, isolation, meltdowns, and anxiety into the shadows.

Entertainers and athletes are celebrated when they embrace the images and expectations of their audience, and judged the moment they display anything different or show human vulnerability. The imbalance created through this dynamic only fosters an environment for chaos, tipping the seesaw to the opposite side and unleashing the darkness of the shadow to openly wreak havoc. Unyielding repression eventually results in volcanic destruction to one's self and others.

Another shadow aspect for celebrities is depression. Depression affects people from all lifestyles and occupations; the entertainment industry is not immune. Muller's article, published in *Psychology Today*, discloses statistical data about depression: "According to Health Canada, mental illness affects approximately 20% of the general population, and the U.S. figure is reported at about 25% by the Centers for Disease Control and Prevention." Neuman, also published in *Psychology Today*, similarly states, "Depression in one form or another is probably the most common cause for referral to a psychiatrist. The affected person is vulnerable to a suicide attempt even if that person has responded well to medication in the past, and knows that. "It is possible to speculate that entertainers are living the dream; therefore, being sad or unhappy is inconceivable. However, that is not the case.

The debilitating disorder of depression is an additional psychological consequence of celebrity and fame. Depression has affected many entertainers and athletes throughout history—from Marilyn Monroe and Marlon Brando to Roseanne Barr, Ashley Judd, and Owen Wilson. *Psychology Today* reported that actress Marilyn Monroe could not beat chronic depression;

at the end of her life, she was under the constant care of a psychiatrist and was prone to mixing prescription drugs with alcohol. Additionally, Roseanne Barr was hospitalized several times throughout her life, and is still undergoing psychotherapy while taking antidepressants.

Furthermore, *Huffington Post* reported Halle Berry's and Owen Wilson's struggles with depression. After Halle Berry's first marriage to David Justice dissolved, she attempted suicide. Berry stated, "I was sitting in my car, and I knew the gas was coming when I had an image of my mother finding me." *Huffington Post* reported on Wilson's episode, stating, "Wilson shocked friends in 2007 when he attempted suicide. The actor had been silently battling depression and drug addiction for years."

Huffington Post lists many other entertainers who suffered from depression. Among these celebrities are Angelina Jolie, Christina Ricci, Catherine Zeta-Jones, Zach Braff, Mandy Moore, Kylie Minogue, Amanda Peet, Uma Thurman, Sheryl Crow, Gwyneth Paltrow, Jon Hamm, Anne Hathaway, Judy Garland, Pete Wentz, Richard Dreyfuss, and Dolly Parton. As for athletes, the online forum *The Sportster* reports many who meet the criteria for depression. Among them are Shawn Osborne, Ricky Williams, Freddie Flintoff, Terry Bradshaw, Stan Collymore, Greg Stiemsma, Frank Bruno, Darryl Strawberry, Larry Sanders, Dwayne "The Rock" Johnson, Oscar De La Hoya, Rick Rypien, Andre Waters, and Paul Gascoigne. The names listed are few, but it is easy to speculate that many more celebrities and athletes experience depressive disorders.

Unfortunately, the discussion surrounding entertainers and athletes experiencing depression does not end with the popular media or *Psychology Today*. Dr. David Giles presented a statement from Keith Floyd's (*TV Chef*) personal experience with depression: "You get frightened to go out. People you'd like to speak to don't speak to you because they're too polite to interfere with your privacy. People you don't want to speak to hound you to death. Everybody thinks you're incredibly rich when you're not. And ... there is no-one to talk to, that is the trouble with being a celebrity. No-one believes you if you say you're lonely or you're worried or you're depressed."

Researchers Smalley and McIntosh argue that fame produces an increase in self-awareness and indicate it can have detrimental effects that can lead to depression and possible suicide. The constant pressure to have a "public self" forces celebrities to have high self-awareness. Heightened self-awareness has deleterious effects. It puts people in a self-evaluative frame of mind. Self-aware people are constantly monitoring their behavior, evaluating how they are stacking up against their own and others' standards and expectations. This heightened self-focus feels unpleasant when people determine that they are falling short of the standard, and the natural reaction is to find a way to escape it. One common escape is alcohol and drug use. Failure to escape persistent self-focus, and the resulting inner voice of criticism, can lead to depression and possible suicide, even if the individual remains famous throughout his or her life (Marilyn Monroe, Elvis Presley).

A great example of this concept is the very public scandal between Brooke Shields and Tom Cruise regarding postpartum depression and pharmaceutical medication. Shields wrote a memoir that was published in 2005, in which she discussed being treated for postpartum depression with medication. Tom Cruise spoke out against Shields' use of antidepressant medication, which brought on a public battle between her and Tom Cruise regarding Shields' choice of treatment for her postpartum depression.

Clark states, "Shields's memoir of depression is interesting because it presents the spectacle of a star writing what could be called a self-expose: in it, Shields confesses to an episode of deep vulnerability and loss of control—a 'breakdown' in her failure to mother, and a resulting dependence on psychiatric medication—in a celebrity system where film stars' public appearances are highly controlled and their screen images invite a distant if admiring identification. Due to continuing stigma attached to any form of mental illness or medication for mental illness, negative publicity is a possible consequence of publication—as happened in Shields's case, when Tom Cruise attacked her use of the antidepressant medication Paxil (instead of more natural alternatives like vitamins) to overcome her depression."

Alcohol, Drugs, and Death

As mentioned by Smalley and McIntosh, finding ways to escape is another common shadow aspect of celebrity and fame. Alcohol, prescription medication, illicit drugs, and death have been a common theme throughout the history of entertainment. As published in *People*, Corey Monteith's premature death shook the entertainment industry and brought forth the dark side of drugs and death. The headline read, "A Life Cut Short: A Troubled Kid Who Beat the Odds and made it Big": "The *Glee* star appeared to have overcome his struggles with drug abuse. Monteith's sudden death at age 31 from a lethal mix of heroin and alcohol leaves friends, family, and girlfriend Lea Michele reeling."

It is impossible to understand the subjective reality of another person unless he or she has a secure container (space)to share, and the tumultuous world of entertainment is not conducive to creating such a space. Unfortunately, friends and family may not even recognize the pain and affliction of darkness their loved one is holding.

In *People*, Tauber interviewed Monteith's family and friends. Webb, an early mentor of Monteith, stated, "He was in great spirits. He looked so healthy. He talked about his recent four-day hike on Vancouver Island's Juan De Fuca Marine Trail, and when the subject turned to his work with project Limelight Society, a nonprofit arts program for kids, his face lit up. Having overcome his own tough childhood, he said, 'The performing arts saved my life once, I want to give back.' "Unfortunately, two days later, Monteith was pronounced dead from a mixture of heroin and alcohol in his room at the Pacific Rim Hotel.

Additionally, Kirk D'Amico, who worked with Monteith on *Sisters& Brothers* stated, "Even though he was part of this machine that is FOX and *Glee*, you never got the sense that he was jaded. There's a kind of Canadian-ness. He had this really charming easiness about him.

Typically people who have drugs in their past seem much darker." As poignantly described by D'Amico, the entertainment industry *has* become machine, and appears to be affecting those working within it.

Similarly, during an ABC News report on celebrities and heroin addiction reported by Colleen Curry, Dr. Joseph Strand of Harvard Medical School and Dr. Jason Jerry, director of the Cleveland Clinic, gave insight on the issue of drugs and death. Strand stated, "In certain professions where there is stress there is a great proclivity to people using alcohol or drugs to get rid of that kind of stress. "Jerry told ABC News that heroin is used in the entertainment industry and that group of individuals is nothing new: "We could have been having this conversation 60 years ago, in the 1950s, when heroin use was huge among jazz musicians." Furthermore, Strand stated, "People who are anxious and depressed or angry and don't like being angry can certainly go to other drugs to have some sense of pleasure." Additionally, Jerry stated, "Many people start taking narcotic painkillers they are prescribed, but then find them habit-forming."

Curry's report for ABC News also discussed actor Philip Seymour Hoffman's death from heroin with suspicion of pharmaceutical drug use. When Hoffman was found dead in his apartment from an apparent heroin overdose, with a hypodermic needle sticking out of his arm and seventy glassine baggies of heroin stored in the apartment, celebrities reacted with shock that such a great talent could be lost to a drug overdose at age 46. Many others were shocked that Hoffman, a respected stage and screen actor, could have hidden a heroin habit. In addition to the heroin in Hoffman's apartment, police also found a slew of prescription drugs, including the blood-pressure medication Clonidine Hydrochloride; the addiction treatment drug Buprenorphine; the ADHD medication Vyvanse (lisdexamfetamine dimesylate); Hydroxyzine, which can be used to treat anxiety; and Methocarbamol, a muscle relaxer.

Athletes also succumb to alcohol and drugs. There is a list of thirty athletes who have struggled with a number of problems. Hockey enforcer Derek Boogaard died in 2011 after mixing oxycodone with alcohol. University of Maryland basketball player Len Bias died of a cocaine overdose. Olympic goalie Pelle Lindebergh died in a drunk driving accident. Football player Todd Marinovich struggled with cocaine, alcohol, marijuana, amphetamines, and LSD abuse. Football player Don Rogers died of a cocaine overdose. Football player Leonard Little killed a woman on a crosswalk in a drunk driving accident. The tragic loss of an entertainer or athlete to an alcohol, illegal, or prescription drug overdose has stunned society many times. Addiction and death seem to be prominent in the entertainment industry, so a state of surprise may just be a way to keep the reality of the issue in the shadows.

In order to highlight the epidemic, Kluwer created a list of entertainers who had alcohol and drugs implicated in their deaths. Iconic singer, Elvis Presley, died of illegal and prescription drug overdose at age 42. Actress and iconic sex symbol, Marilyn Monroe, died of a prescription drug overdose at age 36. Jazz singer, Billie Holiday, died of alcohol poisoning at age 44. Jazz musician, Tommy Dorsey, died of a prescription drug overdose at age 51. Iconic country singer, Hank

Williams, Sr., died of an alcohol and drug overdose at age 29. Actress and singer, Judy Garland, died of a prescription drug overdose at age 47. Singer, Janis Joplin, died of a heroin overdose at age 27. Singer and iconic guitar musician, Jimi Hendrix, died of an alcohol and prescription drug overdose at age 27. Singer and musician, Jim Morrison, died of a heroin and cocaine (disputed) overdose at age 27. Actor, Freddie Prinze, died of an illegal and prescription drug overdose at age 22. Drummer, Jon Bonham, died of an alcohol overdose at age 33. Actor, John Belushi, died of a heroin and cocaine overdose at age 33. Jazz musician, Chet Baker, died of a heroin and cocaine overdose at age 59. Actor, River Phoenix, died of a heroin and cocaine overdose at age 23. Singer and bassist, Kurt Cobain, died of a self-inflicted gunshot wound resulting from drug use at age 27. Comedian, Chris Farley, died of illegal and prescription drugs at age 33. Bassist, Howie Epstein, died of a heroin overdose at age 47. Actress and model, Anna Nicole Smith, died of a prescription drug overdose at age 40. Actor, Heath Ledger, died of a prescription drug overdose at age 28. Pop icon, Michael Jackson, died of a prescription drug overdose while under the care of his personal physician at age 50. Singer, Amy Winehouse, died of an alcohol overdose at age 27. Singer, Whitney Houston, died of a drug overdose at age 48. Rapper, Chris Kelly, died of a heroin and cocaine overdose at age 34. This list of tragic deaths continues, and continues to grow by the year. Most researchers and psychologists have ignored the need for an investigation into the shadow consequences that affect entertainers and athletes.

One study, however, has exemplified the shadow experience of iconic country singer Johnny Cash. This study highlights what may be perceived as shadow elements. In it, Dr. Raeburn points out some lifestyle stressors and addictive behaviors presented by Cash. Dr. Raeburn states, "Johnny Cash hit the road and never really left it. He embraced the touring lifestyle of a professional musician and increasingly felt its impact. He said later, 'The euphoria faded as I began to learn, slowly and often quite accidentally, how the business of music worked.' His marriage to Vivian became deeply estranged, as her needs and those of Johnny's musical career conflicted. She resented this new lifestyle, including the ever-present female fans ... life on the road had its own reality, and that became more powerful over time. Exposure to pills and alcohol increased, as did Johnny's motivation to get high as the tour took its toll on him ... unfortunately, John dealt with the cross-pressures in his life, including his unhappiness in his marriage, by becoming dependent on amphetamines and other substances ... He reported that at one time, he was taking as many as 100 pills a day, amphetamines and tranquilizers."

In addition to alcohol and illegal drugs, it seems as if pharmaceutical drugs have become adventitious to addiction and drug deaths in the industry. In an article "The Nightmare on Pill Street!", Ballard describes the death of Dorothy Dandridge: "On September 8, 1965, Dorothy Dandridge, the first black American to be nominated for an Academy Award for Best Actor, was found dead. The cause was an accidental overdose of Tofranil, an anti-depressant." Similarly, on February 11, 2012, Whitney Houston, renowned singer and actress, was found dead with Xanax and alcohol in her system. Bottles of prescription drugs in her hotel room included Xanax, Valium, and Ativan—all anti-depressants prescribed to treat anxiety.

Furthermore, Ballard argues that anti-depressants, anti-anxiety, and insomnia drugs truly have become "The Nightmare on Pill Street!" In nearly fifty years of prescribing anti-depressants, the results are all too frequently the same: drug addiction, mental impairment, irrational and violent behavior, panic attacks, suicide, and death. An estimated 27,000 people die from accidental drug overdoses in the U.S. every year. That is equal to one death every 19 minutes.

Everything—from eradication of the human factor to loneliness, isolation, anxiety, meltdowns, depression, drugs, and death—has been highlighted, discussed, and exemplified in this section about lifestyle risks of celebrity and fame for entertainers and athletes. As Elvis Presley said, "The image is one thing and the human being is another. It's very hard to live up to an image, put it that way."

Chapter 2

Lack of Personal Space

*"Privacy is not something that I'm merely
entitled to, it's an absolute prerequisite."*

~ Marlon Brando

Loss of Personal Space

Personal space is essential for health and wellness. Dr. David Giles argues, "Evidently this need for privacy—at least a private space that one can enter at will—is a fundamental human requirement." Unfortunately for entertainers, celebrity and fame encroach on the ability to create necessary boundaries—not only for themselves, but for their spouses and children as well. Moreover, entertainers encounter mistrust due to para-social relationships, fan worship, obsession, stalkers, and paparazzi.

Identifying the loss of personal space with celebrity and fame, Smalley and McIntosh indicate an ironic twist to the loss of a privacy that celebrities suffer is the difficulty it causes in making new true friends. Celebrities constantly meet new people: fans, other celebrities, reporters, and so forth. In meeting so many people, it is difficult for them to determine genuineness. Their fame makes it hard to discern who is actually interested in the celebrity as an individual, and who just wants to hobnob with the famous. Additionally, Giles indicates the annoyance that follows celebrity and fame: "A common complaint by celebrities is that they feel as though their 'personal space' is being invaded; after a while the invasion of space becomes too great for celebrities to feel entirely comfortable in public places."

Furthermore, Dr. Donna Rockwell and Dr. David Giles documented concerns regarding personal space for the celebrities' families. The situations conjured by celebrity life become grist for additional concerns about how fame affects the celebrity's family. Can the celebrity protect his or her spouse and child from the darker side of the celebrity experience? For example, one of Rockwell and Giles' participants was heavily concerned with the effect his legacy of fame would have on his 15-year-old son. The participant stated, "I worry about my son, because I don't want him to think of me, because I'm famous, as being any more special than he is. And I wonder sometimes if he's going to confuse fame with worthiness or value as a person, that if he doesn't grow up to be someone who has celebrity or fame, he is somehow not recognized or not worthy of people's respect or admiration. I think a lot of people confuse it. In our whole culture, people confuse it. To be rich and famous—the two words go together. There are a lot of challenges; the family dynamic is complicated by fame."

Drs. Rockwell and Giles further indicate celebrity families often cannot go out together in public and enjoy uninterrupted time without strangers entering the family circle. The famous person's child, baffled by the celebrity social world, may begin to feel anger, guilt, and resentment. Whether it is a fan's friendly slap on the back, a question asking a son if he is planning on following in his father's footsteps, or a daughter's concern that she will never equal her mother's achievements, fame's impact on children worries celebrity parents.

The continuous attention that follows celebrity and fame without abatement or reprieve has been confirmed to be problematic for entertainers and athletes. Similarly, no privacy or detachment from the intrusion and beckoning of others, especially in private moments, has induced psychological distress.

Para-Social Relationships

Besides the invasions of personal space, entertainers and athletes often encounter para-social relationships, which is an additional factor and unique stressor that the general populous evades. A para-social relationship is a single-sided relationship where an individual knows a great deal of personal information about the entertainer or athlete, but the entertainer or athlete knows nothing about the other individual. Horton and Wohl coined the term "para-social interaction" as a label for television viewers' responses to people on the screen. They were among the first researchers to systematically identify similarities between the social situations that media characters attempt to establish for their audience and real-life encounters. Horton and

Wohl also argue that many media "personae" address the viewer more-or-less directly, and that viewers presumably respond to such behaviors just the way they would if the characters were standing in front of them. Conversely, Bryant and Vorderer emphasize the importance of imagination in relation to the development of a para-social relationship.

John Caughey discusses many cases in which people fantasized that they were involved with a celebrity. A well-known example is the story of John Hinckley, who attempted to assassinate President Ronald Reagan in 1981.Hinckley saw the movie *Taxi Driver* and become infatuated with the character Iris. In the film, Iris is a teenage prostitute portrayed by Jodie Foster. Hinckley wrote love letters to her and began to imagine that he was her lover. He eventually started to believe that he could win her affections by killing President Reagan. The Hinckley case reflects an extreme example of dysfunctional imagination common in para-social relationships. More common are para-social relationships in which individuals imagine talking to, or interacting with, media characters.

The illusory connection that some fans feel toward entertainers is vividly authentic within the individual's subjective reality. Rojek states, "The diminution of direct social relations is addressed by what has been called para-social interactions (that is, interactions which occur across a significant social distance—with people 'we don't know'), such as those we enjoy with the celebrities we watch and admire. "It has also been indicated individuals within society compensate for the loss of community by developing an avid attention to celebrities and investing heavily in their "relationships" with the celebrity. It is also speculated that society uses celebrity as a means of constructing a new dimension of community through media.

The effects of a para-social relationship have been displayed many times throughout the years. Exemplifications of para-social relationships have been displayed with the outpour of fan bereavement during the funerals of celebrities like Elvis Presley, John Lennon, Lady Diana, and Michael Jackson. The para-social relationship can affect the individual as it gives them the false belief that they have a personal or emotional connection to the celebrity. Effects of such para-social relationships include fanatical worship, obsession, and stalking behaviors. In effect, these false beliefs due to the para-social relationship can create problematic consequences for the celebrity as the fan acts them out. Jenson stipulates that such a construction is maladaptive and pathologizes the fan-celebrity relationship as it has the potential for the obsessive pursuit of a more direct relationship. Further, para-social interactions are dangerous because they can often be used as a substitute for other kinds of social participation, again carrying the potential for aberrant behavior. Some researchers, including Schickel, stipulate that fandom is an attempt to live vicariously through the perceived lives of the famous. Schickel goes on to assert that fandom is a chronic attempt to compensate for a perceived personal lack of autonomy, the absence of community, an incomplete identity, or lack of power and recognition. A logical outcome of "chronic compensation" is disturbed or obsessional behavior.

Worship, Obsession, and Stalking

A para-social relationship can lead to celebrity worship and obsessional behavior for some fans. Some researchers, including McCutcheon, Lange, and Houran, propose the Absorption Addiction Model to explain cases of celebrity worship. McCutcheon and colleagues propose a model of celebrity worship based on psychological absorption (fostering the need for progressively stronger involvement to feel connected with the celebrity). According to this model, psychological absorption with a celebrity is caused by an individual's compromised identity structure—and is therefore an attempt to establish an identity and sense of fulfillment. The Absorption Addiction Model states that low worship involves individualistic behaviors such as watching and reading about a celebrity. At slightly higher levels, celebrity worship takes on a social character. The highest levels are characterized by a mixture of empathy with the celebrity's success and failure, over-identification with the celebrity, compulsive behavior, and an obsession with details of the celebrity's life.

A number of empirical studies have been conducted on celebrity worship and obsessive behavior that has led researchers to conclude adoration can evoke pathological responses, ranging from vicarious bereavement to erotomania. Some researchers further suggest that beyond the para-social interaction is an abnormal phenomenon whereby individuals with a strong sense of personal identity become virtually obsessed with one (or more) celebrities, similar to an erotomanic type of delusional disorder. The *Diagnostic and Statistical Manual of Mental Disorders 5 (DSM5)* defines erotomania as a delusional belief held by an individual that another person is passionately in love with them.

The *Journal of Developmental Psychology* published findings in 2002 that seventy-five percent of adolescents had a strong attraction to a celebrity and fifty-nine percent were heavily influenced by their favorite star. According to researchers Haynes and Rich, a recent issue of a teen fashion magazine reported on a 16-year-old girl who told of her self-described obsession with a musician and her reaction to the news of the musician's engagement. The adolescent was hospitalized because, in response to hearing this information, she reportedly ran a hot bath and cut herself on her neck, arms, and legs. The teenager stated she was thinking, "She's going to change him if he gets married ... I'm not going to live with that."

A number of studies examining celebrity worship have found evidence that individuals who exhibit celebrity worship behaviors are emotionally or mentally unstable. Celebrity worship has also been linked to depression and anxiety, as well as neuroticism and psychopathology. These findings indicate that celebrity worship is positively associated with neuroticism. Neuroticism is related to anxiety and depression, so the idea of neuroticism as a factor in celebrity worship provides a useful understanding as to why higher levels of celebrity worship are related to poorer mental health. Additionally, significant ego-boundary deficits are operating at this stage of celebrity worship. The Absorption Addiction Model combined with Eysenck's Personality Theory suggests that celebrity worship is firmly rooted in psychopathology and thus may become a serious clinical issue.

Celebrity worship is another unique stressor and shadow aspect of celebrity and fame for entertainers and athletes. Once an entertainer or athlete has achieved fame and the accompanying celebrity status and fandom, danger will inevitably follow. Pursuit by fans can be relentless, and it is relatively easy to obtain the information necessary to stage an encounter with the celebrity. Ferris and Harris point out that fans can access all types of information on their favorite celebrity: "They may glean information from celebrity journalism and fan-related online media about where they can find celebrities working; studios, on-location, charity events, and the like." Additionally, there are maps of celebrity homes sold on every corner, and tickets for bus tours throughout Hollywood, California. The readily available information allows fans to pursue and possibly stage encounters with their favorite celebrities. The pre-staged fan-celebrity encounter creates an imbalance that can leave the entertainer and athlete vulnerable and helpless. Ferris and Harris postulate that once a fan acquires the ability to stage a meeting with a celebrity, the balance of power in the fan-celebrity encounter undergoes a fundamental shift. The security afforded to the celebrity by the scripts and structures of the pre-staged encounters is gone, and the element of chance is removed. As the fan gains knowledge, the celebrity loses protection, and the specter of stalking arises.

The entertainment industry spawns an allure and seductiveness that plays on society's desires, and through marketability and multimedia it awakens the shadow but leaves avidity for more. For some, a glimpse is not enough. This can unlock an individual's obsessive, overly fanatical, and stalking behavior (whether conscious or unconscious).Those with a proclivity for an intimate para-social connection will become consumed and seek to fulfill the fantasy. Lawrence claims that for some fans, there is a belief of an intimate connection with the entertainer. Lawrence states, "If [these fans] met their favorite celebrity, [they would think] the star would understand them and perhaps be their friend, or that their favorite celebrity is truly their soulmate."

Obsession and stalking has become a serious concern in the United States, especially for celebrities. The Bureau of Justice reported that 3.4 million people were reported victims of stalking during a twelve-month period in 2006. Moreover, half of these victims experienced unwanted contact with the stalker on a weekly basis. The Bureau of Justice also states that more than ten percent of stalking victims had been stalked for a period of five years or more.

In 1989, a young actress named Rebecca Schaeffer was murdered by her stalker. It was reported, "Twenty-one-year-old, Oregon-born Schaeffer was the star of the U.S. daytime soap *My Sister Sam*, and had just appeared in her first film, when she was stabbed to death on her own front porch by an obsessive nut. He was a school dropout who became a schizoid-loner, living out his life in his bedroom, building a shrine to Rebecca. He couldn't have her so he didn't want anyone else to either." After the murder of Schaeffer in 1989, California Legislature provided the first legal definition of stalking. According to California Penal

Code Section 646.9, stalking is "the willful, malicious, and repeated following or harassing of another person, which includes a credible threat with the intent to place that person in reasonable threat for his or her safety or the safety of his or her immediate family." Schaeffer's death made the concept and act of stalking a serious concern for the entertainment industry.

Dennison and Thomson argue, "There has been a considerable amount of publicity given to accounts of individuals who have stalked celebrities prior to harming them." The notoriety from the media that stalkers receive by pursuing a celebrity may only exacerbate the desire to continue their hunt. According to research on stalking, there are categories and general characteristics in which individual stalkers may fit. However, due to different upbringings and personalities, each individual may not fit into only one category; in fact, some may exhibit behaviors from multiple categories.

The Judicial Education Center in 2003 described some character profiles of a stalker, which consist of simple obsession, love obsession, and erotomania. The categories are:

Simple obsession: This is the most common type of stalker. The stalker is usually a male and the focus of the stalking is an ex-wife, ex-lover, or former boss. In intimate relationships, the stalking frequently starts before the break-up. The stalking can sometimes result from the stalker feeling that he or she has been mistreated by the victim.

Love obsession: In this type of stalking, the stalker is a stranger or a casual acquaintance to the victim. Nonetheless, the stalker becomes obsessed and begins a pattern of behavior as a means of making the victim aware of his or her existence. High profile examples of this type of stalking include when celebrities or public figures become the target. However, this type of stalking can be focused on an "average" citizen as well.

Erotomania: In this type of stalking, the stalker incorrectly believes that the victim is in love with him or her, and that, but for some external barrier or interference, the two of them would be together. Given that perceived "love" between the stalker and the victim, the stalker can also pose a risk to those persons close to the victim since they may be viewed as "being in the way."

Additionally, The Canadian Psychiatric Association identifies a number of psychological consequences of stalking for the person being pursued. Stalking may indirectly affect a person's ability to work through the many adverse emotional consequences suffered. Stalking has serious mental health consequences, and can affect not only psychological states and interpersonal relationships, but greatly impact occupational functioning.

Public figures are among the most acute cases of stalking. Harvey states, "The most intense form of stalking behaviors are mainly targeted at figures in the entertainment industry; when a fan's interest becomes intense to the point of infatuation, experts describe it as love obsession." Harvey also states, "Most stalkers or those involved in an obsessive interest of one sort or another inhabit a delusional, disjointed, and dysfunctional world. Believing that they can have a relationship with the object of their desire is often the central belief which supports their ongoing obsession; a belief that their victim in turn loves them can often be a further part of their delusional existence." The accumulation of information regarding para-social relationships, fan worship, obsession, and stalking renders immeasurable cause for concern for celebrities.

The death of actress Rebecca Schaeffer focused acute awareness toward the fatal consequences of stalking for celebrities. However, even in 1989 when Schaeffer's stalker took her life, stalking was not a new concept in the entertainment industry. Cases of celebrity stalking had been reported throughout the entertainment industry's history. Entertainers such as singers The Lennon Sisters, actor and comedian Jerry Lewis, musician John Lennon, singer and actress Olivia Newton John, actress Jodie Foster, actress Theresa Saldana, singer and actress Madonna, actor Brad Pitt, and actor Richard Gere all had reported being stalked by a fan. Some celebrity stalking incidents that had been meticulously detailed and documented involved Peggy Lennon, John Lennon, Madonna, and Brad Pit.

Sauerwein discloses that Peggy Lennon's case states that in the early 1960s, she was stalked by Chester W. H. Young, and in 1962 she began receiving inappropriate letters. Young questioned Lennon about "cutie-pie," which was the fantasized baby they had. Young appeared at Lennon's rehearsals, showed up at restaurants, and sat behind her at church. Lennon notified police and a judge sent Young to a psychiatric hospital. However, in 1968 Young was released, and began writing letters to President Johnson threatening to kill him if Johnson didn't help him marry Lennon. The FBI did eventually intervene; however, it did not stop Young from shooting and killing Lennon's father, Bill Lennon, on August 12, 1969. Young was a prime suspect but evaded authorities. His body was discovered on October 11, 1969 in California, in his car.

Sauerwein also describes John Lennon's death as a senseless death that ended an era. On October 20, 1980, Mark David Chapman began his journey to kill Lennon. Chapman decided it was time, and within a week bought a Charter Arms Undercover .38 Special at a Honolulu gun store. On October 30, 1980, Chapman packed the revolver along with his copy of *The Catcher in the Rye*, and boarded a flight to New York City, NY. Chapman failed to purchase ammunition in Honolulu, and while in New York could not find adequate bullets. However, he remedied the situation by visiting friends in Atlanta, GA, who obligingly provided him with five hollow-point .38 SPL cartridges—believing it was for personal protection. On November 10, 1980, Chapman returned to New York City, called his wife and confessed what he was going to do, and had a change of heart after she pleaded for him to come home. Unfortunately, Chapman, who was diagnosed as schizophrenic, continued hearing voices instructing him to kill Lennon. On December 6, 1980, Mark David Chapman returned to New York City. On December 8, 1980, Chapman wrapped the revolver in cardboard to disguise the outline in his pocket, tucked a copy of Lennon's latest album, *Double Fantasy*, under his arm, and that night he shot and killed John Lennon upon the singer's return from a recording session.

More recent incidences of stalking reported by Sauerwein include pop singer and actress, Madonna. In 1996, Robert Dewey Hoskins stationed himself in the entertainment industry hills to watch Madonna with binoculars. The Oregon drifter was obsessed and was convinced she should become his wife. In April 1995, he was spotted on her mansion grounds, and left notes at her gate stating he loved her and she would be his wife for keeps. During one encounter with Madonna's security, Hoskins threatened to cut Madonna's throat. Hoskins attempted to scale the walls of Madonna's property multiple times in order to get to Madonna. During one attempt, Hoskins managed to get over the wall and into the yard, carrying a wooden heart that read, "Love to my wife Madonna." When confronted by authorities, he brandished a gun. As the security guard attempted to wrestle the weapon away, Hoskins was shot and wounded in the arm and stomach.

Similarly, Brad Pitt's stalker, Athena Marie Rolando, began in 1996 with bizarre letters posted on his front gate. One note stated, "If I'm crazy I'm bringing the whole fucking place with me!" Rolando was a teenager at the time, and believed in witchcraft. She cast spells to break up Pit's relationship with Gwyneth Paltrow. On January 6, 1999, police reports indicate that the nineteen-year-old revisited Pitt's home because she had been hearing voices saying, "Go see William," but she couldn't get past the gate and went home.

The next time Rolando followed the voices in her head, she again wrote a note for "William," apologizing for using her magic to destroy his love affair with Gwyneth. Later, Rolando was dressed in only a satin nightgown and bunny slippers when she hired a taxi to take her to Pitt's home. She scaled the nine-foot wall, got into Pitt's home, and after snooping around for ten hours, left a note on the dining room table stating, "Moon; # Riddle...(?) 1. 'You and I (?) here'? 2. 'I am half band but make one complete song.' P.S. Over 3 ½ years ago I place a chant on you and Miss Paltrow to break up. I was young and selfish...I am sorry...I didn't think it would work. And your eyes have haunted me since. Even if Magic doesn't work...I am deeply sorry. AR." After she left the letter on the table, she went up to Pitt's bedroom, rummaged through his clothes until she found some she wanted to wear, put them on, and fell asleep on Pitt's bed. A caretaker found her and called the Los Angeles Police Department.

Paparazzi

The aforementioned elements of invasion of personal space should be sufficient evidence to support the shadow side of the unique stressors encountered by entertainers and athletes. However, there is still the aspect of the paparazzi, which may be perceived by some as legal stalking. Paparazzi, as discussed throughout the media, are photographers who relentlessly follow an entertainer or athlete, seeking that unexpected opportunity to snap a shot of them in an unguarded moment. The market for the paparazzi is highly desirable, which reflects society's obsession with entertainers, athletes, and celebrity culture. Jason Zengerle argues that readers of tabloid magazines view celebrities as friends, and as such, they desire intimate access to celebrities' private lives. Therefore, the tabloids fulfill the fantasy by reporting on the top three life events: weddings, babies, and divorces.

Understanding and achieving success as paparazzi is daunting in itself. However, Peter Howe describes the two main ways in which paparazzi obtain celebrity photographs. Howe states, "There are two main avenues for photographing the things you shouldn't photograph in the places you shouldn't be: gate-crashing and pursuit. The first takes nerve, deception, and the confidence to make people believe that you're supposed to be there; the second takes cunning, knowledge, and the ability to anticipate a celebrity's movements." The explanation of the behavior involved by the paparazzi may lead one to conclude that the celebrity is prey and being hunted. At the very least, the celebrity feels stalked for the purpose of acquiring an image for someone else's income. Barry Levine has been outspoken on behalf of the paparazzi. He is quoted as once saying, "The paparazzi have always been interested in one thing, and that's making money."

Peter Howe argues that the paparazzi have no qualms about their pursuit for images and money. In his book *Paparazzi: And our Obsession with Celebrity*, he states, "I have yet to meet another group that seems so blissfully unconcerned about the opinions of others; for the most part these men and women are perfectly at ease with the way they earn their often considerable living and feel no need to justify their existence." Furthermore, Howe explains, "The job of a highly paid portrait photographer is to transform the stars into icons for the temples of our imagination. The paparazzo, on the other hand, fulfills another fantasy—namely, that these revered beings are just like us underneath their fabulous surface. By showing them shopping, arguing, getting drunk, playing with or slapping their kids, we're allowed the illusion that not only are they people just like us, but that with better luck, or different turn of events, we could be just like them. They may be rich, powerful, and adored, but they also look fat, plain, angry, stupid, or whatever unflattering image of them that is captured by the paparazzo's lens. The paparazzi seek to capture the shadow side of the celebrity, bringing it to the surface whether a celebrity is personally ready to integrate it or not. Forcing anyone to face parts of themselves that they may not be ready for can lead to psychoneurosis and trauma."

Throughout the entertainment industry's history, there have been many incidents of paparazzi turmoil. The greatest publicized paparazzi event was the death of Lady Diana. The high pursuit car chase involving paparazzi that claimed the life of the princess was prominent in the media; every news outlet was airing it. On August 31, 1997, Lady Diana died of injuries from the fatal crash while being pursued by paparazzi through a narrow tunnel. Eyewitnesses claimed that a photographer also took pictures of the wreckage prior to police arrival. The incident created a flood of backlash toward paparazzi.

Another significant social event was the O.J. Simpson arrest for the murders of Nicole Brown-Simpson and Ronald Goldman. Capturing an image of O.J. Simpson in handcuffs was highly sought after by paparazzi. Photographer Phil Ramey explained his pursuit for the image of O.J. in cuffs: "There was only one picture of O.J. like that, when they arrested him; somebody made one frame and licensed it to TV and one magazine group. After doing some investigation, I figured out where they were going to bring him out of the infirmary. Believe it or not, a half hour after we were up there, we saw a van pull up and back in. I knew it was one of the two they used to bring O.J. out. We went into a hover and crept in as close as we could to the jail, without giving ourselves totally away, and with a thousand-millimeter lens with a gyro stabilizer, shot the first pictures and video of O.J. being led away to court in handcuffs."

Many entertainers and athletes are prime targets for pursuit by the paparazzi. A number of actors, singers, and athletes have terrifying stories of pursuit by the paparazzi. Sean Penn, Alec Baldwin, Lindsay Lohan, Britney Spears, Lance Armstrong, Tiger Woods, Kanye West, Justin Bieber, Paris Hilton, Brad Pitt and Angelina Jolie, and Jennifer Lopez and Ben Affleck all have had frightening or contentious encounters with the paparazzi. Athletes have become keenly aware that paparazzi are targeting them now as well. NFL prospect Colt McCoy told ESPN, "You got to be on your guard all the time, no matter where you are or what you are doing, just be smart." Jimmie Johnson, NASCAR four-time sprint cup champion, told ESPN, "[The] magnifying glass is intensifying in the sports world."

Peter Howe tells the story of Ben Affleck and Jennifer Lopez. In 2003, when interest in the marital status of Jennifer Lopez and Ben Affleck reached a state of public obsession, the desire for images produced a death-defying car chase. Howe's report discloses, "Ben Affleck is driving a hundred twenty miles an hour—and I mean one hundred and twenty miles an hour. We thought the police might have been paid off because he's driving at that speed and they're letting him go while keeping all the paparazzi behind. They block off the freeway for half an hour, two cops driving at thirty miles an hour, tons and tons of cars behind them. And Ben and Jen are gone in the distance."

The previous report increases curiosity regarding the paparazzi being the sole participant. Is it possible that it was a publicity stunt to increase desirability and feed the ravenous shadow of society? One may speculate about the reason for obtaining an image, but it does not mitigate the fact that celebrities are in dangerous situations and the human factor is being removed from the equation. One possible reason for such troublesome and dangerous episodes is that tabloids may have difficulty getting advertisement, which would increase the importance of the content and risk-taking tactics to "achieve the shot," so the bottom line can remain profitable. Supply and demand has created the paparazzi, and the more shadowy the content captured, the more profitable the magazine.

An example of this was published in *The National Enquirer*. The magazine published an image of Elvis Presley in his open casket that sold over seven million copies of the periodical. To date, this is *The National Enquirer's* highest grossing sales for any single issue. The craze for celebrity-related gossip has perpetuated a societal shift toward voyeurism. New York-based psychologist Robert Schachter explains, "There's been a whole culture shift in how people are engaged."

The problematic issues involving the paparazzi increased debate regarding protecting the rights of celebrities. A perfect example would be the dangerous encounter with the paparazzi involving Lindsay Lohan. While leaving the parking lot of a restaurant in Los Angeles, the paparazzi began following Lohan.

Eyewitnesses stated that the paparazzi caused a car accident to attain images of the incident. Shortly after the news spread regarding Lohan's encounter, California's Governor Arnold Schwarzenegger signed a law allowing celebrities to collect large damages from paparazzi who harass them. The need for protecting celebrities has increased as society's hunger for vicarious connection has grown. Bentley argues, "The crazy insatiable lust for celebrity in this country is a large driving force in society." One California assemblywoman, Cindy Montanez, stated and reassured that there is a measure directed at those who "break the law in their attempt to get the photograph."

Though entertainers are in the public eye, it does not give license to other professionals to infringe upon their First Amendment rights of privacy. First Amendment lawyer Julie Hilden argues that, "It seems somewhat unfair to say that because a person's gift lies in acting, basketball, or singing, rather than, for example engineering, architecture, or computer science, that he or she has somehow 'chosen' to give up all of his or her privacy."

As for the logistics of privacy law, Shayna Emanuel states, "Privacy is an inalienable right granted by the California Constitution. While privacy laws vary from state to state, California has passed more legislatures protecting public figures than any other, due to the large number of entertainers who make Southern California their homes and the role of that region as one of the centers of the entertainment industry." The Privacy Act of 1974 was passed by the United States Congress following revelations of the abuse of privacy during the administration of President Richard Nixon.

BRIGHT LIGHTS, DARK SHADOWS

Essentially, the law commands that every "United States agency have in place administrative and physical security systems to prevent the unauthorized release of personal records." The act was especially important because it created a new sense of the importance of personal privacy, and its protection.

Adding to Emanuel's argument, a personal interview with Dana Mitchell regarding the Burton Bill of 1998 was conducted. Within the interview Mitchell declared, "The 'Anti Paparazzi Statute' created the concept of trespassing for the purpose of capturing an image for commercial purposes. The bill came in response to a number of embarrassing photos depicting celebrities in the nude. The photos were obtained via telephoto lenses aimed at backyards, hotel rooms, and directly into celebrity homes. The law was designed to discourage invasive conduct by expanding on the existing law and by creating a cause of action directed at setting forth recoverable damages." Additionally, Mitchell disclosed, "The statue tries to reduce aggressive and often dangerous paparazzi-like behavior against private individuals to feed the public's insatiable appetite for sensationalized reporting."

Generally speaking, no other profession encounters the scrutiny and invasion of privacy like celebrities. Bill Gates said it best:" Historically privacy was almost implicit, because it was hard to find and gather information. But in the digital world, whether it's digital cameras or satellites or just what you click on, we need to have more explicit rules—not just for governments but for private companies too."

Chapter 3

Fall from Grace

*"A few names have survived oblivion.
In time, oblivion will have them all."*

~ Marty Rubin

Ageism

Multiple factors contribute to the fall from grace such as ageism, typecasting, coming out, and misdirected child stars. Additionally, due to the image factor, many entertainers and athletes will do anything to uphold their marketability. This includes undergoing cosmetic surgery, stomach banding, extreme weight loss programs, and enhancement avenues. No other industry upholds a more demanding criterion for youth, beauty, and physical ability than the entertainment industry. Evans and Wilson state, "It's so difficult for an actor in the entertainment industry today—you're on your own; when you go up for a role you're either too young, too fat, or too thin, unless somebody already has you in mind."

Ageism and typecasting are two prominent shadow factors in the entertainment industry. When an entertainer or athlete reaches a certain age, or an actor is identified as a particular character (i.e. sex symbol, gangster, or nerd), it can be detrimental to their career. Ageism disproportionately affects female actors and has been problematic throughout the history of the entertainment industry. It is rarely addressed or discussed openly. If a celebrity is not young, beautiful, or physically fit, he or she may struggle to find work. Actress Meredith Baxter explains her theory on the topic: "There are not many 67-year-old women on screen, and that's part of our problem. Women my age—there's more of us around than men my age— we're the predominant part of the populace and we're not represented on television; I don't think they know what to do with us." The music industry is no different. In an interview with *Huffington Post*, Macy Gray (Grammy Award-winning singer) stated that she was told by a record label professional, "I don't know how to get a 40-year-old woman on the radio; if she was 20, 25…"Gray's response to this denial was, "And who would fault her? Everybody knows that a 40-year-old female recording artist is geriatric; while a 46-year-old president is the new kid on the block, a singer over 30 is just a few songs away from the nursing home of music."

"Labeling, "categorizing," and "packaging" are the norms within the entertainment industry. These norms, or rather the failure to meet them, pushes many talented entertainers and athletes to the wayside. An entertainer performs for a living, since it is their career, but aging in the entertainment industry often means unemployment. Furthermore, for those who are in the limelight, surrounded by limitless multimedia access and scrutinizing public conjecture, the pressure can be proliferating. In 2010, Dr. David Gileswrote, "Today, with visual media operating as the principal vehicles for publicity, being beautiful has become a criterion for fame, not a disincentive; fame has evolved into a superficial cultural pursuit that is of little benefit to most of the people who attain it."

Actress Scarlett Johansson criticized the entertainment industry for its poor treatment of aging women. Johansson highlighted the issue in an interview, stating that, "Women kind of wilt as men sort of achieve as they get older, like wine or whatever; it's like, 'Oh she is past her prime and she can't play a sex symbol.' It's just a preconceived notion about women in general and particularly in this industry. It's a very, very vain industry."

Ageism in the entertainment industry has become so apparent that members of the entertainment industry developed The Industry Coalition for Age Equity in the Media. The coalition is backed by the Screen Actors Guild (SAG), Women in Film, the American Federation of Television and Radio Artists, and the California Commission on Aging. It is known that entertainers and athletes are in demand throughout their twenties, but as they age, they begin to lose ground. This affects female athletes and women in the entertainment industry disproportionately.

To get a better understanding of ageism in the music industry, Trini Trent outlines the core causal factors. Trent states, "We've seen dozens of female artists gradually lose steam as they age into their 30s before experiencing a dramatic decline in their commercial success when they turn 40. As if labeled with an expiration date, these women suddenly become irrelevant to their primary music markets when they approach that fateful age." Trent continues his discussion, "The entertainment industry, specifically the areas of music and film, is the primary provider of visual products for consumers demanding a constant stream of fresh and exciting content. That demand affects everything and everyone, therefore placing an incredible strain on artists to constantly reinvent themselves. Unfortunately, it is impossible for any act to keep up with the ever-changing trends in entertainment, and female artists feel the brunt of that pressure. Think about it: To whom do we look for the hottest trends in fashion? Whose music videos get the most airplay? Whose 'hottest' lists in magazines gets the most attention? That's right, women are always in the glare of the media spotlight, and they are expected to remain cusp of everything new—which seemingly can't be done by aging acts. Furthermore, the problem has been exacerbated as a result of social media, specifically on sites such as YouTube, on which visuals can be overanalyzed by both fans and critics eager to spot every possible 'flaw'."

Fighting ageism is an uphill battle, and the media does not contribute to its demise; it only further illuminates the adverse effects of aging. Melissa Dittmann reports that a longitudinal study conducted by psychologist Becca Levy indicates that age stereotypes are often internalized at a young age, long before they are even relevant to people; even by the age of four, children are familiar with age stereotypes that are reinforced over a lifetime. Levy also argues that fueling the problem is the media's portrayal of older adults. At a senate hearing, Levy testified before the Special Committee on Aging about the effects of age stereotypes. Also testifying was Doris Roberts (Emmy award-winning actress), who is in her seventies. Roberts stated, "My peers and I are portrayed as dependent, helpless, unproductive, and demanding rather than deserving; in reality, the majority of seniors are self-sufficient, middle-class consumers with more assets than most young people, and the time and talent to offer society." Levy further noted that the value that the media and society place on youth might explain the growing number of cosmetic surgeries among older adults.

As Becca Levy points out, many entertainers choose to undergo the knife to keep that youthful appearance in hopes to remain marketable and continue with their careers. As for athletes, they sometimes implement enhancement drugs to meet the expectations of the public, while at the same time denying the accusations. This raises an important question about our society. Why does society create such unattainable expectations from a human being? Why does society then harshly judge athletes and entertainers who fold to the pressure to meet societal expectations?

Moreover, the entertainment industry emphasizes physical beauty so much that the reality TV show *The Swan* was produced and aired on television. *The Swan* required contestants to undergo cosmetic surgery and then compete in a pageant. Sometimes the outcome of surgery is abominable and creates problems, which can lead to psychological issues.

Melissa Dittmann reports that a study on plastic and reconstructive surgery found that "Patients who are dissatisfied with surgery may request repeat procedures or experience depression and adjustment problems, social isolation, family problems, self-destructive behaviors, and anger toward the surgeon and their medical staff. Additionally, Chandramita Bora reports, "Patients opting for plastic surgery, especially cosmetic surgery, should be very well aware that the results they obtain might differ from what they were expecting before they went under the knife. Sometimes these procedures can leave behind scars that may not go away with time. This can have a lasting psychological effect on patients, plunging them into depression. People suffer from intense regret and anger toward themselves and the doctor for a procedure gone horribly wrong, not to mention embarrassment and criticism they might face from friends and family."

The media thrives on publishing the mishaps of the entertainment industry because the public devours it like candy. Bryann Mannino reports that if the romance flick-loving world hadn't fallen so wildly in love with the face that used to belong to Jennifer Grey (*Dirty Dancing*), then perhaps her transition would have had less of an effect on her career. Though Grey's aesthetic appearance remains pleasing, unfortunately the rhinoplasty ("nose job") that she hoped would help her during casting calls relegated her mainly to made-for-TV films. There are a number of entertainers who report having cosmetic surgery with unsatisfactory outcomes. Comedian Scott "Carrot-Top" Thompson had a botched eyebrow lift, Botox injections, lip plumping, and a laser peel that turned out poorly, and he is now the butt of many other comedians' jokes. Actor Mickey Rourke had a facelift, upper eyelift, and hair transplant that turned out so poorly it nearly destroyed his career. *Guns and Roses* front man Axl

Rose had cheek implants and a facelift that turned out poorly. Actress Nikki Cox had cheek and lip implants that turned out poorly.

Few entertainers will openly disclose if they have undergone plastic surgery, let alone discuss unfavorable outcomes. However, one actress who has spoken publicly about her botched cosmetic surgery is Tara Reid. During an interview with *CBS News*, Reid discussed her breast augmentation and body contouring procedures. For her breast augmentation, Reid states she originally requested full B cups, but received C cups instead. Shortly after surgery, Reid noticed deformities around her nipples that never went away. Reid's body contouring surgery left her stomach lumpy and unnatural-looking. After the botched cosmetic surgery and resulting deformities, she received a barrage of negative press. Reid states that after this, she went to therapy for one year to get help regain her confidence. As previously disclosed, the pressure of youthfulness by the industry has the potential to create psychological distress.

The embodiment of beauty is not the only limitation for remaining employed in entertainment industry. Preserving the spotlight as a working entertainer and athlete is demanding emotionally, cognitively, and physically. The industry is ruthless and it will devour whoever does not serve it. Even though entertainers and athletes go to great lengths to remain a viable candidate for new ventures, some may still be limited. Take typecasting, for example. For an entertainer, typecasting is a silent death because the artist is not recognized for their full potential, and is not able to actualize the entire spectrum of their talent. Once an artist has been typecast, it is very difficult to break away from the image the industry has created and society has chained them to.

There are a number of examples of historically famous typecasting in the entertainment industry. Marilyn Monroe, an actress, became known and typecast as an iconic sex-symbol .John Wayne, an actor, became known and typecast as the iconic rugged cowboy, a symbol of the American west. Ron Howard, an actor and director, became known and typecast as the charming boy next-door. Jennifer Aniston, an actress, became known and typecast as the girl next-door. Angelina Jolie, an actress, became known and typecast as the tough sex-symbol. Jim Carrey, a comedian and actor, became known and typecast as the extreme comic. Will Ferrell, a comedian and actor, became known and typecast as the self-deprecating man-child. Darius Rucker, a singer, became known as the ultimate adult contemporary mainstream artist. Garth Brooks, a singer became known as a country-western singer.

For some entertainers, typecasting may be an unfortunate, inevitable outcome. Typecasting has been discussed by professionals of the Raindance Film Festival: "Actors get typecast. It's a harsh reality, but a reality nonetheless; it happens. And by typecast I mean, after the breakthrough role that jumpstarts their career they (usually) get offered other roles, and a big percentage of such roles will inevitably be somewhat similar to the one they are known for."

A specific example is the typecasting of Jennifer Aniston. Jason Serafino speaks bluntly and unflinchingly about Aniston's typecasting. Serafino reports, "Every role she takes is about as safe as they come. She's only found in cookie-cutter romantic comedies where she plays the lovelorn lead that needs to either A) move on to another man, or B) fight for the one she's after. The problem is that the roles she chooses are often so similar that we, as a society, should no longer care about whether or not Aniston finds love." Other entertainers who have been typecast have been actor Danny Trejo, who continuously is cast as the tough-guy, villain, or antihero. Actress Michelle Rodriguez is typecast in tougher roles as a tomboy. Actor Hugh Grant is inevitably cast as an English romantic leading man. Another type casted artist is singer Darius Rucker, who was inundated with a lot of animosity when he tried to crossover from mainstream to country, and singer Garth Brooks, who took a huge risk trying to cross over from number one hit-selling artist in country to his fictional character of Chris Gains to enter the pop charts. Typecasting may limit the breadth and depth of a celebrity's creativity and ability. However, it is still not the only brick wall an entertainer can run into.

Coming Out

An additional injurious factor for an artist or athlete's career is "coming out" and homophobia. In fact, twenty years ago, coming out as gay or lesbian never would have happened. Currently, the climate for LGBT actors is improving; however, it continues to be controversial.

In 2014, actress Ellen Page (*Juno*) joined a growing population of entertainers who openly admitted they were gay. Page disclosed, "I suffered for years because I was scared to be out; I'm standing on the other side of that pain." There are many risks, personally and professionally, for people who come out. Corrigan and Matthews argue in their research that, "Perhaps most sobering among the risks of coming out for sexual minorities is bodily harm; the news media regularly reports on hate crimes based on sexual orientation."

However, for celebrities who are already scrutinized by the public, "coming out" may result in a magnified deleterious effect on multiple levels A recent study on the sexual minority populous reported that 41 percent of a sample of lesbians and gay men reported being victims of a bias-related crime, and another approximately 10 percent reported an attempted bias crime against them.

Throughout the history of the entertainment industry, confirming one was gay would destroy a celebrity's career. Pomeratz states, "In another era, a famous person admitting to being gay would have been the end of his or her career. Movie stars under the thumbs of big studio contracts regularly married and had children just to continue a façade of heterosexuality." In other professions, sexual preference is a personal matter and not a topic of public discussion. In fact, if individuals in other industries are denied employment or experience prejudice due to sexual preference, it warrants legal proceedings. However, the entertainment industry has been able to use publicists and professional fixers to create the illusion that entertainers and athletes are not gay in order to meet the criteria of desirability for society. Coming out in the midst of a public career is not easy for an entertainer or athlete who wants to embrace their authentic self fully. In fact, full disclosure may result in sabotage and lack of employment. Pomeratz states, "Actors are different. They have to disappear into their roles on the big screen. And like it or not, most studio executives are going to take a long pause before hiring a gay actor, especially when that actor is young and maybe hasn't already created a hetero image that sticks in people's brains."

Corrigan and Matthews confirm the previous concept by stating, "Of even greater concern, disclosing one's sexual orientation may translate into job and housing discrimination." The stigma around being gay in the entertainment industry is legitimate. Sexual preference other than heterosexual has been portrayed as a shadow issue, which has been masked throughout the history of the industry. However, bringing the shadow element into the open may allow an entertainer or athlete to integrate it into their conscious, and bring it forth into the collective unconscious of society.

Recently, a well-known athlete named Jason Collins came out as gay in an interview with *Sports Illustrated.* Collins' coming out opened an avenue for reporter Tyler Cowen to write about athletes and entertainers who come out of the closet. Cowen states, "Presumably if an up-and-coming actor comes out, it is hard for that actor to get roles as a romantic lead and perhaps as an action lead in a "buddy movie" as well It seems well-known female celebrities find it easier to mix coming out with continued career success...I am happy to hear about Collins. But we will be seeing much more progress when up-and-coming handsome actors, shooting for big the entertainment industry roles, also come out as gay. That to me still seems far away." In an industry that professes liberal views, it is vexing that homophobia continues to exist. Other athletes who have come out as reported by the *Huffington Post* have been: Gus Kenworthy (Olympic silver medalist), Keegan Hirst (rugby player), Mason Darrow (Princeton football player), and Yusaf Mack (professional boxer), who told Fox 29, "I'm gay. I'm tired of holding it in, it is what it is. I live my life, I'm gay."

Jodie Foster's coming out speech at the Golden Globe Awards stirred controversy around the topic of homophobia and the financial bottom line in the entertainment industry. The upheaval from Foster's statement allowed Geoffrey MacNab to report, "Foster's speech has caused huge commotion in the entertainment industry. It came days after a story on entertainment industry news and gossip site *The Wrap* quoting director Steven Soderbergh as saying that *Behind the Candelabra*, his new biopic of entertainer Liberace, was turned down by every studio as 'too gay.' The budget was modest ($5m), the cast was impressive (Matt Damon and Michael Douglas), but the entertainment industry simply didn't want to know...the real issue here, of course, is economics. Gay and lesbian directors and producers, studio heads and supporting actors can be open about their sexuality as long as it doesn't get in the way of the work. It is with the leading players that the Omerta code applies most strictly."

Actor Rupert Everett shared his concerns, and advised other actors to refrain from disclosing their sexuality. Reported in the *Daily Mail*, Everett stated, "Aspiring actors stay in the closet as it could harm their career. It is not that advisable to be honest. It's not very easy. And, honestly, I would not advise any actor necessarily, if he was really thinking of his career, to come out... The fact is that you could not be, and still cannot be, a

25-year-old homosexual trying to make it in the British film business or the American film business or even the Italian film business. It just doesn't work and you're going to hit a brick wall at some point. You're going to manage to make it roll for a certain amount of time, but at the first sign of failure, they'll cut you right off. And, I'm sick of saying: 'Yes, it's probably my own fault.' Because I've always tried to make it work and when it stops working somewhere, I try to make it work somewhere else. But, the fact of the matter is, and I don't care who disagrees, it doesn't work if you're gay."

Pressures for keeping silent do not stem solely from the industry; fans have also turned on entertainers who have openly admitted they were gay. When young actress Raven Symone from the Disney Channel show *That's so Raven* came out as a lesbian, it created a huge uproar by fans. Many of her fans used their Twitter accounts to voice that the news ruined their childhood. Fans insinuated that the realization of the entertainer's sexuality destroyed the impact that the Disney show had on their development. The public may choose to avoid people who have come out, and the social disapproval may negatively impact the self-esteem of people who are out.

Other entertainers who felt the effects after admitting they were gay included Ellen DeGeneres, who lost support from advertisers for her television show. Religious groups pressured networks to drop her, and ABC and Disney put a disclaimer at the front of her sitcom stating some themes may be inappropriate for children. Similarly, singer Lance Bass was ostracized and marginalized by the people from his hometown of Mississippi, and he received death threats.

The dynamic of an entertainer's and athlete's sexual preference can have an impact on their personal and professional success. Exemplified public persecution, which the media exacerbates, is just another unique stressor that entertainers are confronted with. Coming out is another slippery slope toward the fall from grace. However, it is not the last.

Child Stars

Another obvious and painful public display of the fall from grace is the decline of a child star. Most people are unaware of the gated community right outside Hollywood, California named Oakwood Toluca Hills. This community was set up to house the almost famous, and it is where many child stars stay while pursuing stardom. Not only does it seem that parents and the entertainment industry profit from young talent, but also businesses within the community.

Jake Halpernin describes the Oakwood Toluca Hills community as being home to the famous and almost famous. Halpernin states, "Within the walls of this sprawling enclave one can find a furnished apartment, a rental-car agency, a general store, a dry cleaner, a beauty salon, a tennis shop, a car wash, and a busy schedule of weekly activities for kids, including a spirited karaoke session every Wednesday night. The complex was built in the early 1970s, and its many boxy buildings and orderly footpaths give it the look of a quickly constructed college campus. Still, Oakwood's facilities— including 1,151 apartment units—are in impeccable condition. Oakwood bills itself as the ultimate in one-stop shopping for actors—especially child actors—who need somewhere in the entertainment industry to stay until they are discovered. The list of celebrities who have passed through Oakwood over the years includes Hillary Swank, Jennifer Love Hewitt, Queen Latifah, Ricky Martin, Frankie Nunez, Aerosmith, and Jamie Foxx just to name a few. Oakwood has made a concerted effort to attract child actors by creating a special website establishing a weekly schedule of events for kids, and inviting agents and managers for the 'youth market' to come and speak on a regular basis. Oakwood courts these children and their parents, who are out-of-towners, primarily because they are willing and able to pay a premium to live in a family-oriented place with a national reputation as a steppingstone for budding stars."

However, the avenue to child stardom does not begin and end here; it is merely the gateway to the slippery slope of many youthful tragedies that enter the entertainment industry scene. Many child stars epitomize the fall from grace, and have been critically wounded by the industry. Evans and Wilson state, "Those that enjoyed childhood fame were vulnerable to problems like suicide, underage sex, and addiction to drugs and alcohol. Given such a strange role reversal with their parents whereby they 'parented' their own parents, both financially and emotionally, it is hardly surprising that the lives of child actors are a unique psychological case study in themselves."

A few examples are Mackenzie Philips and Corey Feldman. Philips disclosed the choice she made to live with her mom or dad. Philips claims, "Dad thought for a minute: 'Here are the ground rules,' he said. 'You have to be home one night a week,' he said, 'and if you stay out all night, never come home in the clothes you left in. A lady never wears evening clothes during the day. It's cheap.' That was it, the house rules. There was no phone curfew here. There was no curfew whatsoever. My brother and I were together again. Jeffery wasn't afraid to ask for drugs. I wasn't afraid to ask for money. We got both. When it came down to it, the choice had been: Live with my mom in a condo in Tarzana, do homework, heed my curfew, and follow Lenny's rules, or live with my dad in a mansion, hang out with the most famous movie stars and rock stars of the day, and have no rules whatsoever."

Similarly, Corey Feldman was also exposed to the shadows of the entertainment industry life. In his biography, Feldman explains, "One day, River and I were hanging out with a member of the crew, an assistant to the sound engineer, when we spotted a bong perched high up on a shelf in the closet. River pointed, and we both giggled...I still can't believe we managed to convince that guy from the sound department to let us smoke, but he did eventually pull down the bong, pack the bowl, and gave us each our first hit. Additionally, I had long since discovered a sort of nightclub on the outskirts of the town, set up specifically for underage teens. It was located inside an old, abandoned warehouse; local kids would congregate along the cement ramp outside until the doors opened sometime around 8 pm."

Time and again, tragic stories have been told about child stars. Becoming a celebrity and coping with fame during the developmental years without specialized guidance may be overwhelming—to say the least. Researchers Evans and Wilson, 1999, discuss that,

BRIGHT LIGHTS, DARK SHADOWS

"Many found it difficult to form emotional attachments later on in life."

Actress Diana Serra Cary explained that for her, marriage had represented a psychologically imperative "comeback." She said, "It must prove to everyone— most of all ourselves—that, washed up though we might seem at eighteen or twenty, we were intelligent adults who could make a success of the most important career in life—matrimony. I believe the terrible sense of failure that we child stars carried over from adolescence made the failure of marriage a far more devastating experience than outsiders might imagine it to be. Divorce only re-projected on a still wider screen the original break-down of our childhood image. I for one had no idea of who I was or where I was going. All I knew was who I had once been and that was a tough act to follow."

Historically relational issues of child stars have been apparent. Many entertainers married multiple times, and some fled the limelight to get away from the image of the characters they had played in hopes to have a life. Evans and Wilson state, "Other child actors married several times—seven in the case of Mickey Rooney, and eight in the case of Elizabeth Taylor."

Richo reports in his writing on the shadow that, "The shadow of childhood is in the abuse and neglect we may have suffered at the hands of our parents and the secrecy that may have surrounded it. Every trauma of early life becomes a drama in adult relationships unless it is mourned and healed. This drama is the deepest shadow of adult intimacy. We repeat our past and do not even realize we are doing it...When our early needs were not fulfilled and still remain unmourned by us, we may not feel safe enough to show our authentic choices, characteristics, attributes, and feelings, since we might thereby lose approval. This creates a false self. Yet only a true self can establish and maintain an intimate relationship and a healthy self-image."

To find and achieve happiness, some child stars fled from their past—such as Heather Ripley, who moved to Ireland to avoid attention after *Chitty-Chitty-Bang-Bang*. Former child stars have opened up about their subjective reality during the years of fame and celebrity.

Michael F. Blake stated, "Speaking as a former child actor I can confirm that we don't retire. We are forced out of a job by growing up. We are then put into the unenviable position of having to choose a new direction for our life and career. We got very little career advice— some child actors might have gotten advice from older actors or directors on a personal level, but none ever got any advice on a general level from the unions (SAG or AFTRA) in Los Angeles. The industry should do more for child performers, but sadly, they never will. Some go on to use drugs, rob dry cleaners, appear on TV chat shows and generally say to the world feel sorry for me, I'm no longer important...Make no mistake about it, being a child actor can be tough. Your career is pretty limited time-wise. And it can play on your psyche when you are no longer needed by the film and TV industry."

As an adult, Heather Ripley (*Chitty-Chitty-Bang-Bang*) stated, "The stress of the whole ordeal traumatized me so much that I have Attention Deficit Disorder, which I didn't have before the film. I can't hold down a job or keep relationships together, I have very poor organizational skills, I suffer from mood swings, anxiety, paranoia, stress, depression, and alcoholism and have been through a couple of periods of drug addiction. My parent's divorce was doubly difficult for me as it was partly caused by them being separated for fourteen months during the filming, which I internalized a lot of blame for, and subsequently I was effectively alienated from my entire family with the exception of my father and grandmother. I have only recently got to grips with most of my problems after six years counseling at the Findhorn Foundation, and have re-established a good relationship with my mother, who did not speak to me for ten years. Kids should absolutely not be encouraged by their parents to seek fame at an early age. Fame, in itself, has little benefit and many disadvantages. I think that if I had continued as an actor—though I am a damn good actor—I would be dead or insane."

Experiencing too much fame too fast at an early age has serious consequences, and Ripley's proclamation is a poignant illustration of a shadow outcome. Rapport and Meleen stipulate, "Celebrity is a non-normative childhood experience; celebrity children respond to life stress as do other children. There is no paradoxical nature to these children; the talent that placed them in the limelight does not include special resistance to stress, and they do not specially thrive on pressure and competition." It has also been suggested that even brief exposure to fame can induce negative consequences, resulting in feelings of diminished sense of control, loss of trust, and powerlessness. Child stars are isolated from traditional educational settings, and when success transpires, it equals the pressures of fame, financial incentives, and rigid schedules with set calls and media appearances. Furthermore, few children achieve recurring roles, which means added stress to continue working.

Many factors may contribute to the fall of a child star such as mismanagement from parents, inundation, scrutiny from the media and society, the environment of the entertainment industry, and unlimited access to anything the child may want. Unfortunately, there are many child stars who exhibited destructive behavior throughout their careers in the entertainment industry. Some examples follow.

Actor River Phoenix (*Stand By Me*) was one of the more tragic incidents; he died at age twenty-three from a speedball overdose. Actress Drew Barrymore (*ET*) smoked her first cigarette at age nine, drank at age eleven, got high by age twelve, was hooked on cocaine as a pre-teen, and had been to rehab twice before the age of fourteen. Actress Jodie Sweetin (*Full House*) was severely addicted to crystal meth, and actor Brad Renfro was found dead of an overdose of heroin at age twenty-five.

There are many more examples of tragic events and child stars who lapsed into the void of the entertainment industry. The downward spiral of child stars was depicted well in an article for *Campus Squeeze*. The author states, "Being a child actor is strange. You get all these sweet privileges that other kids your age never get; like getting to party in an LA nightclub at age thirteen or having a birthday cake the size of a Buick. But it also has a very dark side. Once your cuteness wears off, no one will cast you in a movie, so the next thing you know, you're boxing Steve the Dell guy on a reality show for money, and shaking hands at a Subway in Miami just to feel famous again."

Unfortunately, the bright lights and dark shadows of celebrity and fame have proven to be a high price for young stars. Children more often than not want to please the adults around them, and the pressures from the industry, producers, managers, and parents may be overwhelming. Based on the aforementioned evidence, child star tragedies are very real, and an end is nowhere in sight.

Chapter 4

Observation and Integration

*"Shadow work is the path of
the heart warrior."*

~ Carl Jung

Advocacy

Most scholarly material has focused on demonstrating that celebrity and fame have a disadvantageous effect on society. Ferris and Harris, in their 2011 research, state that, "Many scholars and pundits treat celebrity and fame as matters of pathology or commodification." Behavioral sciences, such as psychology, have discussed the dangers that come with the rise of Celebrity Worship Syndrome. However, little has been studied about individuals working in the entertainment industry and its effect on the entertainers and athletes themselves.

Challenging the current perspectives, and encouraging a more comprehensive account of celebrity and fame that focuses on the effects from the entertainer's and athlete's viewpoints, is a good starting point. Focused observation on the shadow side of celebrity and fame for entertainers and athletes is imperative for a better social understanding of the phenomenon. Reviewing celebrity and fame from the shadow lens enables one to identify aspects that are unconscious to allow for integration, self-actualization, and wholeness. Robert Bly reports, "The shadow energies seem to be a part of the human psyche, a part of its 360-degree nature, and the shadow energies become destructive only when they are ignored."

Richo stipulates that our personal shadow "is the dark side of our healthy ego. It is our neurotic, inflated ego, of which we are mostly unaware. The neurotic ego is the part of us that is caught in fear and in attachment to control and entitlement. It is the FACE—Fear, Attachment, Control, and Entitlement—that we show to feel safe. The ego does not know its first name, Fear, but loves its last name, Entitlement. The ego is the face we are trying to save in 'save-face' and do not want to lose in 'losing-face.' This arrogant ego can be our way of disavowing our vulnerability to the conditions of existence: things change, nothing lasts, things are not always fair, pain is part of life, we are alone. Such harsh conditions are the shadow side of our human existence but 'Not Evil' in themselves. This happens best with a beginner's mind that is no longer in the grip of a frightened or demanding ego."

Looking through the shadow lens will contribute to identifying external shadow material—such as projections from other people, cultural shadows, and collective shadows—so that the entertainer or athlete will not be the sacrificial lamb and will be able to confidently disown what is not theirs.

A glimpse of the collective shadow of fame was expressed by a singer named Gary Numan:"The benefits of fame exert such a pull that there is a tendency for a celebrity to dwell only on the positive aspects of fame, so that the negative aspects arrive unexpectedly and suddenly." Numan's comments seem to support this theory: "Becoming famous was nothing like I expected it to be...I often equate it to losing your virginity. You think about it forever and when it happens it is almost an anti-climax. You feel deeply unprepared for it and you really have to learn how to do it." Giles continues by stating that it is clear there is a need for celebrities to be better prepared for fame, beyond the contributions of financial advisors and influences of record companies. Some preparation might even extend to friends and families of the famous, whose role becomes increasingly important as fame exerts its pressures.

From afar, it would seem that being famous would be an optimal state, and maybe when an entertainer has first skyrocketed to fame it is a welcomed rush. However, more times than not, the elation fades as it becomes difficult to cope with what the shadow of fame and celebrity bring forth. With the help of the media, great fame can be actualized and many stars begin to resent the constant intrusion, pressures of the public glare, and storm of fans taking over their lives.

In previous sections, the unique stressors were outlined: lifestyle risks, lack of privacy, and the fall from grace. These unique variables, and the way they are encountered, are something the general populous does not encounter within their daily lives—and never will. Let's review Robin Williams' death in response to the severity of the consequential effects of the shadow of fame and celebrity.

Alana Horowitz reported for *Huffington Post*, "Beloved actor Robin Williams was found dead on Monday, police reported. The apparent cause of death was suicide by asphyxiation, authorities said. According to his publicist, Williams had been battling severe depression and spent time in rehab as recently as July. "Williams' suicide emphasizes the urgent and critical necessity for a specialized focus within the psychological field for preventative measures to help entertainers and athletes. Williams' death also illuminates the stigma and fear of societal judgment for a celebrity if he or she were to disclose encountering psychological issues.

Maybe Williams, who was known for making so many people laugh, was lost and drowning behind his comedic persona. Entertainers are human too, and each experiences the same emotions, concerns, and fears that every person in society faces. Ben Collins quoted for *Esquire* a role that Williams fully embraced: "I used to think the worst thing in life was to end up all alone. It's not. The worst thing in life is ending up with people who make you feel all alone."

The tragic event also poignantly brought forth the pressures and effects fame and celebrity have on the family members as well. It was reported that Williams' daughter had to terminate her Twitter account due to rude comments and photo shopped images of her father's deceased body.

Dough Gross of CNN reported that "Twitter is looking to revamp its user-protection policies after Zelda Williams, the daughter of comedian Robin Williams, was run off the social site by abuse in the wake of her father's apparent suicide." Del Harvey, Twitter's Vice President of Trust and Safety, said in a statement: "We will not tolerate abuse of this nature on Twitter. We have suspended a number of accounts related to this issue for violating our rules and we are in the process of evaluating how we can further improve our policies to better handle tragic situations like this one. This includes expanding our policies regarding self-harm and private information, and improving support for family members of deceased users." Zelda Williams abandoned her Twitter and Instagram accounts the Tuesday after, saying at least two people were sending her photo shopped images of her father's dead body and other disturbing messages—some blaming her for her father's death.

The incident inflicted upon Williams' daughter clearly indicates that there is a social component to the effects on celebrity family members as well. Glen Collins of *The New York Times* discussed the unique problems of celebrity families with Dr. Harold Cronson, psychiatrist at the Timberlawn Psychiatric Hospital in Dallas, Texas. Cronson stated, "In a sense these families have been overlooked by many in our profession. Family members are often reluctant to seek help, and when they do they may be treated by those who are unaware of their very special problems. The sense of social isolation and loneliness caused by attempts to protect themselves from repeated intrusion by the public and news organizations, and a constant concern about confidentiality and trust, growing from painful experiences with those who have exploited family members." The tragedy of Williams' death will not be the last, because there is no indication that celebrity and fame as well as celebrity culture has peaked.

Furthermore, Turner stipulates that there seems to be no end in sight: "Celebrity content has become fundamental to the news media in the twenty-first century. The growth of new media has generated new ways of representing, consuming, and producing celebrity while online journalism—especially where it is developed as an additional platform for the mainstream print media—has also had an expansionary effect. One revealing detail is the growing trend for the so-called 'quality' newspapers to foreground celebrity stories and photo galleries in their online editions when they would be reluctant to identify with something as down market as celebrity news in their print editions. At the other end of the spectrum, in the zone of the paparazzi and the shock-horror scandal sheets, celebrity journalism has also found new vehicles through which to infiltrate mainstream media markets.

"While relatively anodyne television entertainment news formats such as *E! News* have been screened for many years, a significant recent development is TMZ's migration from its niche as an edgy, muck-racking, explicitly disrespectful, celebrity gossip and news site to become high-rating prime-time cable television program. TMZ's rise to industry respectability, notwithstanding the fact that it has stuck to its original style and focus, demonstrates that even the most shameless exploitation of celebrity culture can find a place within the mainstream television schedule today. Inherently spectacular, closely tailored to contemporary news values, endlessly iterative and renewable, celebrity news is perfectly built for rapid news-cycles, short-form news, and for the contemporary media's preference for entertainment-based content."

Considering there is no end in sight to the interest and desire for fame and celebrity—which can be conveniently achieved through traditional entertainment industry avenues as well as the world-wide-web, mass media, and reality TV—it would imply that acknowledgement of the issues are in order. It's time to talk about the elephant in the room.

Based on the evidence gathered so far, it is inconceivable that there has been little investigation of the effects of celebrity and fame on entertainers, athletes, their families, and those working in the industry. Additionally, it seems incomprehensible that there has not been a specialized focus developed within the psychological profession that specializes in helping artists, athletes, their families, and those working in the industry (i.e. writers, producers, directors, crew, etc.),given all the unique stressors that occur.

Advocating for the Future

Some aspirations are to have wellness centers on every studio lot, with access to trained "entertainment psychologists" who will help entertainers acquire coping strategies to meet and walk through the needs and unique stressors encountered within the industry. Additionally, seminars for parents who manage their children's career—which will be implemented by trained entertainment psychologists—can be provided at studio lots to help the family navigate through the process of child stardom. Furthermore, an on-call crisis center (Fame 911) and agency for travel entertainment psychologists can be developed and implemented to address any situation that may occur on location or on tour as needed.

Robert Downey, Jr. has lived out-loud and walked through the entertainment industry ringer since his youth. He has also openly traveled into the depths of his darkest shadows, faced his demons, and returned as an integrated functional adult. Downey, in his autobiography, discusses his epiphany about harmonizing fame and celebrity: "I have become more Harrison Ford about the whole thing. I'm separating my life and my career. I get a kick out of being in the public eye and it feels like my real life because I spend so much time in it. But I have this aesthetic distance now too because I know about the dangers ... I know how unhealthy my self-love and my desire to be in the spotlight have been." When working with the shadow, as Downey exemplifies, unmasking it is essential to self-actualization and spiritual growth.

Chopra, Ford, and Williamson describe in their research how to unmask the shadow as Downey exhibits: "All of our habitual behavior stems from an experience or experiences in the past that led us to create particular interpretations about ourselves. From those interpretations certain thoughts were born, and these thoughts made us feel a particular way about ourselves, often a negative one. Our desire to distance ourselves from these unwanted feelings drives us to find ways to make ourselves feel better, thus the birth of our self-sabotaging behaviors. If we explore our behavior patterns—especially those we don't wish to repeat—we always uncover a shadow aspect of ourselves that we are trying to hide or cover up. The repetitive patterns we find ourselves trapped in always echo back to us feelings that accompanied the original wound. Then, in a great cover-up, we create patterns of behavior that ultimately reinforce the wound rather than giving us the relief that we seek.

"Every time we find a behavior that threatens our peace of mind our happiness, or our safety, we are implored to heed the call of our internal world and explore the root cause of our behavior. When we do, we will unveil an aspect of our shadow. It doesn't have to take a year or a lifetime. It can take five minutes of radical honesty to unravel a pattern from our past. If we find an impulse in ourselves that we unknowingly hid, we have the right to bring it into the light of our awareness, forgive ourselves and others for the pain we experienced, and break free from the self-defeating behavior. To make peace and break the cycle, you must now confront the distaste you feel for the notion of being selfish and expose the judgments you have held toward all those who you have deemed selfish in the past.

"You must admit to the negative connotations you attach to the word 'selfish' and be willing to see that the way you are interpreting that word is limiting, disempowering, and rigid. You must look to see when you decided or were told that selfish people were bad and wrong. You must become willing to open your heart to the selfish part of you and forgive all those who have reflected back to you that being selfish is bad. You must accept the dualistic view that being human comes with both the healthy dose of selfishness and an equal dose of selfishness. If you are unwilling or unable to find a positive view of being selfish and insist on keeping it in the shadow, you will continue to be held, clinched in the pattern of behavior that has you continue to neglect what is important for your individual growth and the fulfillment of your soul's desires."

Zweig and Abrams argue that to become whole, one must integrate the shadow by confronting opposites: "In all areas of psychic life we must confront our opposites and re-own them. By progressively confronting one's opposites, it becomes more and more obvious—and this point can hardly be repeated too often—that since the Shadow is real and an integral facet of the ego, all of the 'symptoms' and discomforts that Shadow seems to be inflicting on us are really symptoms and discomforts which we're inflicting on ourselves, however much we may consciously protest to the contrary. It is very, very much if I, for instance, were deliberately and painfully pinching myself but pretended not to! Whatever my symptoms on this level may be—guilt, fear, anxiety, and depression—all are strictly the result of my 'mentally' pinching myself in one fashion or another. And this directly implies, incredible as it may seem, that I want this painful symptom, whatever its nature, to be here just as I want it to depart. Thus, the first opposite you might try confronting is your secret and shadowed desire to keep and maintain your symptoms, your unaware desire to pinch yourself. And may we be impudent enough to suggest that the more ridiculous this sounds to you, the more out of touch you might be with your Shadow, with that side of you that is doing the pinching."

While Downey was caught-up in the unhealthy cycle of repetitive, self-destructive behaviors, he could not step back long enough to be the observer of his shadow. A pivotal moment, however, arrived for Downey where he was able to embrace his shadow-self. He did not ignore, or try to rid, his shadow and desire of self-love and being in the spotlight. Instead, he acknowledged it and met it with unconditional openness to harness the knowledge to integrate it with the light—to empower Self and become whole and harmonized. By confronting his shadow, Downey began recognizing the shadow patterns, situations, and people within his life that were contributing to his self-destructive and negative, confirming behaviors. In recognizing these patterns and behaviors, he was able to let go of the detrimental conditioning, people, and situations, and open to a functional self-love and acceptance, allowing healthy patterns to emerge. Downey has integrated positive people and patterns that support, uplift, and love him unconditionally to help him maintain his new way of life. Downey is just one success story of a child star who can forewarn of the pitfalls of celebrity and fame and help up-and-coming talent.

Bridging the Gap

Providing an open dialogue between entertainers, athletes, and psychologists to develop awareness for wellness within the industry will benefit many people. Giles' research states, "Celebrities may need a psychologist to help them through the first year or two of fame, particularly to deal with the public, and to deal with press attentions, especially when it is negative (bad reviews) or intrusive (paparazzi nuisance)."

Additionally, research with actors can be conducted regarding the shadow elements left behind from playing a character or role. It is claimed that actors are taught to hone the skill of empathy so that he or she may enmesh themselves with their part. By doing so, the actor may deeply feel all the emotions of their character to authentically represent and convincingly convey the experience.

Since that is the case, there should be an investigation into the detrimental or shadow residue that may linger within the psyche and unconscious from embodying a character. For example, the shadow effects that the character of the *Dark Knight* may have induced upon Health Ledger—or Charlize Theron's role in the movie *Monster*, where she portrayed a female serial killer suffering from antisocial and personality disorders.

Moreover, the loss of fame or the possibility of never reaching one's expected goal of success is another critical area that needs to be examined and addressed. Entertainers and athletes need to develop coping skills and a "plan B" to survive the fallout of celebrity and fame. Developing and implementing skills such as emotion-focused, cognitive-focused, physical-focused, solution-focused, spiritual-focused, calming, and breathing-focused coping strategies can help the transition. The three basic reactions to the loss of fame are clinging, reinventing, and downward spiraling.

Smalley and McIntosh claim, "*Clinging* is often seen in individuals famous for playing a particular character or embodying a certain persona. After the loss of fame, the celebrity finds it difficult or impossible to gain recognition apart from that role. Thus the celebrity clings to the role, incorporating it into his/her life, sometimes successfully, sometimes unsuccessfully (i.e.

Bob Denver, of *Gilligan's Island*, never seen onscreen without an iconic white hat; until his recent death, many people did not know his real name). *Reinventing* is where an individual completely rejects the former public self in favor of their original core-self. They do not attempt to capitalize on their former fame by becoming their public self. They instead find a new life and new vocation."

Smalley and McIntosh continue their discussion: *Downward spiraling* is the most publicized loss of fame. Here loss of fame leads to despair, potentially resulting in some combination of depression, substance abuse, and suicide. These individuals can be from many 'fame backgrounds,' from briefly famous to years of worldwide fame. Nonattainment of valued goals causes people to self-focus, and under these circumstances, self-focusing is unpleasant. The problems this class of celebrities faces that arise from self-discrepancy are worsened by self-consciousness. Self-consciousness is an important aspect of any person's life, but especially that of the celebrity.

As for creating and implementing a "plan B" from the start, Evans and Wilson stipulate, "It is better to have a 'plan B' for dealing with life after fame, rather than stumbling into it. Good examples of second careers are buying and dealing in property, investing wisely, opening an interesting company, going into production, writing a book, becoming a chat-show host, or that other essential career of starting a family."

The vast knowledge and potential positive outcome from working with and researching professional entertainers and athletes are limitless. Not only will developing scientific research toward the development of entertainment psychology help the world of entertainers and athletes on a micro level; it will also allow the psychological industry achieve a deeper understanding of human behavior and help society on a macro level.

Raeburn points out the benefits on a micro level by stating, "Efforts to acknowledge and identify risks and develop interventions in the performing arts have been left largely to private practitioners and individual organizations operating without the benefit of shared information or an organized field akin to sports medicine." Goldstein claims the macro level by stating that, "We are all actors to some extent, trying different roles as we interact with others."

This is merely the beginning of a much-needed advocacy for an open dialogue between the two worlds of psychology and entertainment. The intent is to encourage wellness to minimize the detrimental effects and consequences occurring within the entertainment industry.

Chapter 5

Shadow to Light

"Truth will ultimately prevail where there is pains taken to bring it to light."

~ George Washington

Fast Forward to Present Day

Currently, an upheaval in the entertainment and sports industries has occurred, and slowly the shadowy veil is rising. It seems as though entertainers and athletes are coming forth, fearlessly calling out the dark matter. As stated in previous chapters, child stars have faced injustice and abuse, ageism is being witnessed and discussed, and currently the casting-couch issue is verified and brought out into the open. This is just a scratch on the surface of what the industry projects upon the humans working toward their life's dream and aspiration. It would seem that embracing ones' talent has a higher price to pay in these industries opposed to any other industry, such as aspiring to be a doctor or lawyer. The thick smoke and warped mirrors are strategically placed in a way to mask the darkness while giving power and illumination to the illusion of light. The glitz, glamour, persona, and recognition of celebrity and fame may appear to be a star shinning bright, but in reality it is more of a beautiful nightmare.

One hidden nightmare is the deep seeded pedophilia issues eroding the underbelly of Hollywood. Corey Feldman spoke with CBS reporter Andrea Park about his new project to expose Hollywood's pedophilia secretes. Feldman stated, "I told everybody a few days ago that I had a plan to hopefully bring to light what is happening in the world of entertainment as far as perverts and pedophiles and all the topics we've been discussing."

It seems, however, that Feldman has not been the only child star preyed upon by those in the industry. In an interview with *Lord of the Rings* actor Elijah Wood, *The Daily Beast* reported Wood's knowledge of child abuse in Hollywood: "Clearly something major was going on in Hollywood. It was all organized. There are a lot of vipers in the industry, people who only have their own interests in mind."

Furthermore, a headline of FOX News Entertainment read, "Everybody Knew Corey Feldman and Corey Haim were 'Passed Around' to Hollywood Pedophilias." Jessica Sager, a reporter from the *New York Post*, interviewed Feldman: "With me there were some molestation and it did come from several hands, so to speak, but with Haim, his was direct rape, whereas mine was not actual rape. I believe Haim's rapist was probably connected to something bigger and that is probably how he has remained protected for all these years." Sager's report went on to include that people knew this was occurring, and she even went as far to include what Feldman reported to *The Hollywood Reporter*: "Ask anybody in our group of kids at that time: They were passing us back and forth to each other. [Alison Arngrim] from *Little House on the Prairie* said [in an interview], 'Everybody knew that the two Coreys were just being passed around'."

Multiple entertainers are coming forth with allegations of pedophilia in the entertainment industry. CNN covered the story on Anthony Rapp's disclosure of sexual misconduct by Kevin Spacey. Rapp came forth saying that Spacey was making sexual advances toward him at age fourteen in a private room. Shortly thereafter in response to Rapp's accusations, Spacey tweeted, "I honestly do not remember the encounter. It would have been over thirty years ago. But if I did behave then as he describes, I owe him the sincerest apology for what would have been deeply inappropriate drunken behavior, and I am sorry for the feelings he describes having carried with him all these years."

Spacey's tweet, for some, could be perceived as more of a dismissive "Oops, I was drunk, my bad," rather than a sincere apology. When harm has occurred to another—consciously or in a drunken state—one would think that, when a response is given, it would not include the words "inappropriate drunken behavior."

The entertainment industry is not alone on the account of pedophilia encounters; accusations within the sports industry of doing harm to athletes have been raised too. Turning now to the sports industry, Dr. Larry Nassar—the former Michigan State University and USA Gymnastics Team doctor—was accused and convicted of sexual abuse.

The Huffington Post reported that one hundred and forty women came forth, and days before Nassar's conviction, the question posed by survivors was, "Why does no one seem to care about their story?" Survivor Morgan McCaul, in her interview with *Huffington Post*, stated, "I remember when the Penn State scandal was talked about at length for months and months and even years. This is nearly five times the size and no one knows about it."

The New York Daily News headline appeared in bold letters: "Olympic Gymnast McKayla Maroney says Team Doctor Repeatedly Molested Her." The report went on to discuss the allegations: "Two-time Olympic Medalist McKayla Maroney revealed on Wednesday that her former USA gymnastics doctor sexually abused her for seven years—starting when she was just thirteen."

Maroney was not the only one to encounter abuse. Reported by *New York Daily*, multiple women over the years had been assaulted by Nassar under the guidelines of "medical treatment." Maroney shared that, "It seemed that whenever and wherever this man could find the chance, I was treated. It happened in London before my team and I won the gold medal, and it happened before I won my silver."

The most heart-crushing statement within the *New York Daily* report was Maroney's experience on the trip to Japan: "She said the worst of the abuse took place during the 2011 World Championship in Japan, when she became a breakout star. Maroney reported that Nassar gave her a sleeping pill on the flight to Tokyo, and she woke up in his hotel room, once again getting a treatment. 'I thought I was going to die that night,' said Maroney."

Corey Feldman coming forth about his pedophilia encounters and his aspiration to develop a documentary seemed to help others embrace inner courage and their voice to speak up. Another group, The 5 Browns—a known classical piano ensemble—has come forth to tell their story and support the fight for the Child Victims Act.

The headline of the *New York Daily* stated, "Utah victims say N.Y. kid abuse laws too weak, join fight to enact Childs Victim Act." The family group brought charges against their father, and then their manager, Keith Brown, for sexual abuse. As reported in the *New York Daily*, when the Brown siblings were looking into bringing sexual abuse charges against their father, they learned the New York state laws would not work. Instead, they chose their home state of Utah. The Brown siblings support this act because of their own journey through abuse: "Once I realized how unfortunate the laws are here and how little recourse children survivors have here, it just made sense for us to join the fight," Desirae Brown told *New York Daily*.

Also supporting the Child Victims Act, Corey Feldman at the New York state capitol, as reported by the *New York Daily News*, confronted senators who are opposed to passing the Childs Victim Act. Feldman, actor and survivor of child sexual abuse, Sarah Powers-Barnhard, former U.S.A. volleyball player, and other advocates urged senate to allow a vote on the bill for victims of child sexual abuse to seek justice as an adult. Feldman walked away heavyhearted, stating, "They don't seem to even want to hear it, it's like they already made up their mind."

Feldman did not quit there, though. He wrote a letter and left it for Senate Majority Leader John Flanagan, giving details of his own child sexual abuse that occurred in Hollywood. Feldman wrote, as indicated in the *New York Daily News*, "I ask you to think of all the children in your life ... and consider who needs your protection most. It is these innocent children, or the coaches, priests, teachers, and relatives betraying our trust to abuse and traumatize them?"

Johnathon Schaech (actor, writer, and producer) has also come forth to speak of the dark side of the industry, and shared his demons and self-medicating behavior after the molestation by Director Franco Zeffirelli. Schaech's disclosure sheds some light on the concept pondered within the psychology industry for years: Is disorder and dissonance innately within these entertainers and athletes, or in fact is the industry inducing and exacerbating these issues?

Schaech told *People*, "I was raised properly. My parents are good parents. They love me, I was just too ashamed of that moment, I was ashamed of being dyslexic, and both those things caused me to shut down and define a big part of me. That shame manifested in so many different ways. I medicated myself so I wouldn't feel so bad about myself and to try to handle my low self-esteem."

Schaech further described the encounter and expressed that, "Whether I talk about it or not, it's still going to be inside me. But as people bury their abuse, it breeds sickness. The problems in my life had a lot to do with that moment. A predator found me and gave me this great opportunity, and took advantage of me. I was molested, touched, groped, I was verbally abused. He beat me down to do that. The psychological part was key—and he made sure he set it up. I had been innocent and although I thought I had all the answers, I didn't have any."

The previous expressive descriptions of how healthy life was before celebrity and fame for Schaech, and how the erosion of toxicity by the industry played a role in the negative emotions and behaviors, may help the psychology industry and society see the detrimental effects experienced by entertainers and athletes. Schaech expressed to *People*, "It is not okay for a producer to use his power to take advantage of an actress. It's not okay to take the innocence away from a child, a boy. I don't care if you are twenty-two, or twelve, a man, or a woman, it's not okay to take away innocence because you are in a power position to do so. You have to face that thing that is evil inside you or you will continue it onto the next generation."

Schaech nailed the issue of the shadow, and the necessity to awaken the demon, acknowledge it, bring it forth, and integrate it to start the healing process of self and others so the next generation may be free of past generational issues—so all may begin to expand and self-actualize on a clean slate.

As described multiple times in previous chapters, it is mandatory for the integration of the shadow to be completed in order to become whole and self-actualized. In these cases, the shadow is detrimental, but it is wise to note that the shadow is not always negative. Shadow may be positive too, and it is a part of the natural world and order of things. It still needs assimilation into self to become whole.

To hear that these unthinkable behaviors have been going on throughout the years in both of these industries is terrifying. We, as a society, should also acknowledge that this is not just happening to females, but also males within both industries. We, as a society, need to witness and stop turning our heads away in denial from the unspeakable. We need to allow our youth to know it is their right to talk about their pain without inducing the fear of blame and shame. The times need to transform from the past mentality where it was once said, "What happens in the house stays in the house," to a current frame of thinking, which allows our youth to feel safe to speak out and seek justice when he or she is hurt or touched inappropriately.

Furthermore, in this day and age, there is also the Internet where children and young adults may fall prey to predators in the industry. Corey Feldman, in his interview with Seth Abramovitch from *Hollywood Reporter*, warns of the dark side and the "Growing, not shrinking dangers of Internet-era child predators in Hollywood, a place where adults have more direct and inappropriate connection with children anywhere else in the world."

There are some preventative measures, one being Sentrypc, an award-winning computer monitoring software company. Statistical data gathered by Sentrypc indicates that "approximately twenty-five percent of children who encounter a sexual approach or solicitation told a parent or adult [Crimes Against Children Research Center]; one in thirty-three youth received an aggressive sexual solicitation in the past year, this means a predator asked a young person to meet somewhere, called on the phone, or sent correspondence or gifts through the US Postal Service [Your Internet Safety Survey]; and seventy-seven percent of the targets were fourteen and older, and twenty-two percent were age ten to thirteen [Crimes Against Children Research Center]."

The aforementioned shadow issues may be boiling to surface in an attempt to heal and expand toward a healthier era and zeitgeist. Integrating the shadow begins with acknowledging the repressed hidden truths and working through the fears, emotions, and mechanistic blockages that repress them. The discussion in Hollywood does not stop with actors or athletes; an elite industry respected writer-director has also come forth to disclose knowledge of the pedophilia issues.

Oscar-winning writer-director Paul Haggis came forward to suggest Hollywood is still hiding reliable allegations of pedophilia. Jay Syrmopoulos—journalist for the Free Thought Project—shared a quote from Haggis: "It is not an innocent place and never has been. Most of this behavior has been aimed at women, but I am sure that former child stars such as Corey Feldman and Corey Haim, who have both made allegations in the past that no one took seriously, are worth considering too."

Heather Graham is also witnessing a need for change. She recently told *Los Angeles Times*, "Well, I worked on *License to Drive* with Corey Feldman and he just came out [forward] and said that he was being molested during that time. That is so disturbing. During that time, no one would've talked about that, people wouldn't feel confident enough to tell the story. I think now people are like, 'Let's just be honest, let's just be open.' There's not that sense of shame about things."

There is a need to bring what is lurking within the collective unconscious out, and integrate it into the collective conscious in order for healing to begin. "I think that is what is happening right now in our culture because people are going, 'You know these things happened to me, and I think the person that did them to me is screwed up. I don't feel it's my fault. That's a massive cultural shift," Graham expressed to the *Los Angeles Times*.

There are many avenues for perpetrators and pedophiles to encounter their victims. Parents, teachers, and society need to educate our youth of the pitfalls and tactics these people will use to lure them into an unsafe environment and situation. As adults, we need to speak truth to our youth, warning them of the psychological, behavioral, and language phrases that a predator may use to make them feel safe. There is a need to unveil and reveal the manipulative psychological mindset that predators and pedophiles work from to lead an innocent into a false sense of security and gain access to their mind, body, heart, and soul.

Our youth need to understand how a predator or pedophile may try to gain access and relations with him or her .Our youth need to understand that a predator may also use threats of harm, fear-based machinations, or shame-based manipulations to keep him or her from telling another adult. These are all harsh realities, yet they are still realities of our day and age. Youth need to be mentally armed and knowledgeable of the threats lurking in their world.

As indicated in earlier chapters, celebrity and fame comes with unique issues and stressors that the general populous does not encounter. There is an imbalance of the shadow within the entertainment and sports industries, which has lurked in the dark and been exacerbated over the years. It is time to acknowledge, face, integrate, and put into place preventative health, wellness, and ethical measures. People in the entertainment industry knew about the encounters of pedophilia and did nothing.

While interviewing with *The Guardian*, Haggis stated, "Were people covering for pedophilias too? We have to think that may have happened as well, because no one speaks out about being abused to benefit their career. I find it particularly terrible that people had their dreams held to ransom in that way." The question at hand, other than if those involved will be prosecuted, is should the people who knew and withheld information of these unlawful and illegal acts be held responsible too? How does one decide? Where are the mandated reporters in these industries?

From the research and interviews done throughout the years on celebrity and fame, it may be reasonable to consider that the entertainment and sports industries consist of people who have leveraged their status, power, and rank to knowingly and willingly manipulate and harm others for personal gain. By doing so, those within the industry—those acting on these behaviors and those keeping the secrets—are holding the aspirations and dreams of innocent, hopeful entertainers and athletes hostage. These acts not only point to the conclusion of unethical and unlawful action; they could be construed as premeditated and malicious behaviors.

Many children and young adults have fallen prey to abuse, and been violated in these industries. How many more will face abuse before society, and those aware in the industry, demand justice for the victims? What has to take place to weed out and eradicate the people who are harming children and young adults behind closed doors? Where is the Hollywood Crime Watch Team ready and willing to uncover and investigate the injustice occurring in these industries? Can such a team be implemented, and be supported by the appropriate legal jurisdictions as a viable investigative body? What licenses and regulations need to be implemented to create this team?

Adults are not immune to the manipulative acts and power play within these industries. Ageism, coming out, and cosmetic surgery to continue marketability were such issues in previous chapters. One issue not addressed in previous chapters, but always whispered about and lurking in the shadow, is the infamous casting-couch idea. Folklore, Wives' Tale, or Fact, many have wondered through the history of the entertainment industry.

The concept of the casting-couch blusterously and forcefully erupted into the light in order to be acknowledged and discussed, forcing integration into the collective conscious. Best described by *The Metro News*, the casting-couch is the place where sexual favors are demanded by a powerful film producer or director from aspiring actors or actresses who want a role in their production. This subject erupted on the entertainment scene when a plethora of accusations about Harvey Weinstein's misconduct over the years was made known by multiple actresses.

The Metro News continued to report that, in part, the victims feel trapped into silence. They feel powerless against the abuser who could end their career or smear their name, and makes open threats to do so. The "you'll never work in this town again" cliché became a cliché for a reason. *The Metro* further reported the very first incident of sexual assault took place in 1920, when Roscoe 'Fatty' Arbuckle was found beside actress Virginia Rappe who was screaming in pain on the bed. She accused him of raping her.

This, yet again, is not the norm for society and exemplifies the unique stressors that entertainers and athletes face within the industry they work in. Turning a blind eye and looking the other way is only feeding the industry and powerful, while disarming, debilitating and victimizing the "human beings" with the talent. Reported by *The Metro News*, professionals in the industry have spoken about the "machine" that exists to silence victims of sexual assault in the form of PR smear campaigns, lawsuits, threats of being fired, or blacklisting.

Without the talent, where would the industry be? Stop for a moment, and really think about that. The entertainment and sports industries could not exist without the talent that provides the energy for the machine to run. Therefore, what if entertainers and athletes were to stop and revolt, demanding that the wizard come forth from behind the curtain—meaning, everything harmful and hidden revealed? Would that shift the shadow enough to bring it into the light to begin integration and establish preventative measures?

After the Weinstein incident and upheaval, the *New York Times* listed seventy-one men within the entertainment, media, and sports industries for sexual misconduct. Reporters from the *New York Times* wrote, "In what appears to be a seismic shift in what behavior is tolerated in the workplace, a cascade of high profile men, many in the entertainment and news media industries, have since been fired or forced to resign after accusations of sexual misconduct that ranged from inappropriate comments to rape."

The following is a short and non-limiting list, reported by the *New York Times*, of the men accused for sexual misconduct: Gordan Edelstein – artistic director of Long Warf Theatre, accused of sexual misconduct with four women, including groping, masturbating, and forced kissing; James Rosen – Washington correspondent at Fox News, accused of sexual harassment of three female colleagues; Mike Germano – chief digital officer at Vice Media, accused of sexual harassment of two women; Don Hazen – journalist and executive director at Alternet, accused of sexual harassment of five female employees, including unwanted advances, explicit emails, and pornographic photos; Charles

Dutoit – conductor and artistic director of the Royal Philharmonic Orchestra, accused of sexual assault of four women; Jerry Richardson – owner of the Carolina Panthers NFL team, accused of sexual harassment of female employees; and the list goes on and on.

How have these types of behaviors and maneuvers been pushed aside, going unnoticed for decades, in an industry that is so publicized and in the eye of the public? Seriously, again, sit back and ponder that concept for a minute. If this were any other industry, where there are regulations and laws of ethics in place, and HR departments to uphold equilibrium, would this have gone on as long as it has? These are industries greatly idolized and desired by the public, as well as sought after by those with talent—so it seems not too far of a stretch to do everything possible to eradicate harmful effects.

A different aspect, and maybe not so damaging, of the shadow of entertainment is the ageism issue, also mentioned in previous chapters. Jane Fonda is currently opening up and beginning a conversation regarding the ageism issue in Hollywood. Quoted in the *Washington Post*, Fonda stated that "Ageism is 'Alive and Well' in Hollywood." Fonda explained how it is more difficult for women in the industry due to the perceived pressure of societal youthfulness for females, and the idea that males just get better as they age. "With women, it's all about how we look. Men are very visual, they want young women. So, for us, it's all about trying to stay young," she said.

Fonda continued telling the *Washington Post* that she knows a few women who have aged in front of

Hollywood's eye, but that she has not been able to embody the idea of aging naturally. She openly and honestly admitted to getting plastic surgery to help her with the aging process to remain marketable to benefit her career and remain viable: "I am brave in a lot of ways, but not that one. And I need to work, so I had some plastic surgery. It's not like it's too much—it's not like you can't see my wrinkles, right? But I think it probably bought me a decade of work." Fonda's open disclosure regarding her experience as an aging female within the entertainment culture was a viable representation to advocate for change within the industry.

That said, in what other industry would one feel the need to have plastic surgery to continue their marketability and continue working for another decade? This yet again exemplifies the pressures and expectations put on the artists working within this industry. Categorizing ageism and all the other subjects discussed as unique stressors induced by the entertainment and sports industries seems to be fair.

Further supporting news was reported by Angel Watercutter in *Wired*, with a headline that read, "Tina Fey nailed it: Hollywood has a serious ageism problem." Within the report, a survey by USC's Annenberg School for Communication and Journalism analyzed that "1,256 speaking parts in 25 movies received best picture Oscar nominations from 2014-2016 ... only 148 characters (12 percent) of those characters were 60 years of age and older—and, of those 148 characters, 78 percent were men and 22 percent were women."

BRIGHT LIGHTS, DARK SHADOWS

An additional topic, which burst on the scene in the sports industry and not addressed within this book, occurred with Jonathan Martin's Instagram post regarding bullying and the effects years later. *Yahoo News* reported that, "After a troubling Instagram post led to his former high school being closed for a day, former NFL offensive lineman Jonathan Martin has checked into a mental health facility." An image was sent from Martin's Instagram with a shotgun, shell casings, and writing that stated, "When you are a bully victim & a coward, your options are suicide, or revenge." Additionally, written on the image of the shotgun handle was the name Miami Dolphins, and on the barrel the name Harvard Westlake.

Bullying has always been a detrimental issue and has been in the public eye for a while now. These behaviors inflicted upon our youth as they transition into adulthood do not just go away; they have lasting effects. Indicated by the Bureau of Justice Statistics, "There were 31 schools associated violent deaths from July 1, 2010 through June 1, 2012. In 2012, among students' ages 12-18 there were about 1,364,900 nonfatal victimizations at school, which include 615,600 victims of theft and 749,200 victims of violence."

Bullying is another avenue of interest to explore as pressures that contribute to stress for entertainers and athletes. Whether it is an athlete who is the star on the team, or the one who holds the team back, or the kid at school who does not fit in because he or she has different behaviors or mannerisms that do not fit into the norm yet enhance their artistic performance and unique self. What is the spectrum of healthy or unhealthy? Who really gets to decide that, since all humans have their own spectrum from Shadow to Light? Is there a point for the introduction of preventative techniques? What will those techniques and tools look like?

Currently, there is a petition that advocates for a new division within the psychology industry called Entertainment Psychology. This petition will need one percent of the American Psychology Association members to sign it to create a specialized entity. After accumulating the needed signatures, the American Psychology Association will evaluate, debate, and vote upon the need and benefits for the new division.

Entertainment Psychology would be devoted to answering some of the above questions, and the scholarly and practical study of the psychological aspects of the entertainment and sports industries, which hold the promise of significant benefit to the field of psychology, our clients, and society at large. Practitioners, researchers, and students interested in Entertainment Psychology as a legitimate discipline could seek specialized education by the division and thereafter may help those in the entertainment and sports industries.

This new division would comprise mental health, entertainment, and sports professionals, its mission rooted in the recognition of the development of entertainment psychology as integral to the development and maintenance of entertainment, sports, and psychological well-being. Through a collaborative, organized effort, developing theory, research, and evidence-based interventions will result in a rich addition to the science and profession of psychology.

Entertainment Psychology would be a multi-faceted domain that extends into numerous areas relevant to contemporary life and the field of psychology, including ego strength, behavioral development, memory and cognitive functioning, emotion regulation, and personality and psychosocial development, as well as traditional psychotherapy. The division seeks to more formally unite and serve these diverse but often related areas of interest by supporting the advancement of Entertainment Psychology research, education, training, and practice.

The previously mentioned issues and stressors throughout this book may foster an environment for a state of emotional, mental, physical, and spiritual symptoms—not to mention neurosis such as anxiety and/or depression. Not only do entertainers and athletes deal with the constant strain and obstacles of their profession; they are set up for struggles by the industry in which they work (as mentioned throughout this book).

After reading the collection of information, will society and the psychology industry dismiss the detrimental unique stressors induced by the entertainment and sports industries? Or will advocating for measures to be taken and specialized treatments to be developed cause that to occur? Imploring new preventative strategies and regulations, informed and co-created by those working within the industries to bring awareness to the unique issues encountered, may help the up-and-coming entering the work force.

Maybe the industry of psychology, after reading the material set forth, will see a need for preventative programs and a specialized division. It does seem as if the standard pre-existing methods are not working for the lifestyles described throughout this book. The system seems to be broken, and a population of "human beings" are falling through the proverbial crack.

All the information presented leads to the support of a new division and the petition posted with the American Psychological Association (APA) advocating for the development of a specialized focus called Entertainment Psychology, which will be devoted to the scholarly and practical study of the psychological aspects and unique stressors encountered within the entertainment industry. A documentary and/or televised series highlighting and developing constructive dialogue around the shadow aspects of the entertainment industry—with testimonies from entertainers, athletes, psychologists, and other professionals throughout the industry—is an additional aspiration.

Entertainers and athletes are more than what is portrayed in the news and tabloids, on television, and on the big screen. Whether there are pre-existing psychological conditions that are exacerbated by unique stressors or psychological, distress-induced conditions from the unique stressors of the entertainment industry, it is time to advocate for preventative measures as well as health and wellness throughout the industry.

About the Author

Mimi Amaral is the pioneer for Entertainment Psychology, an aspired division with American Psychology Association. She holds a Doctorate Degree in Clinical Psychology with a Bachelor's Degree in Psychology and Business.

Mimi is an author advocating for awareness of the shadow of celebrity and fame and domestic violence toward men. She is a journalist for Splash Magazine and the SOP, covering and promoting entertainment, fundraising, and awareness events. Furthermore, she has designed and patented (with her business partner) a medical device that is an innovative medication delivery system.

Mimi is a speaker and advocate for RAINN (Rape, Abuse, and Incest National Network). She is also a keynote speaker bringing awareness to Entertainment Psychology and abuse toward men.

Mimi also consults and empowers people to be their authentic self and manifest their aspirations. Why, you may ask? "I lived it," she replied.

Recognized, Interviewed, and Articles by: APA Monitor, Division Dialog, and two times with Judyth Piazza (American Perspective Radio Interview).

Mimi's first published work was her dissertation: "Bright Lights, Dark Shadows: An Integrative Literature Review of the Psychological Consequences of Celebrity and Fame for Entertainers," which is currently being proposed for a documentary.

Her most recent work is this book: *Bright Lights, Dark Shadows: The Shadow Side of Celebrity and Fame.*

Mimi lives in California. Her aspiration in life is to advocate for those who are not seen, and to encourage everyone to be their authentic self while participating in their own wellness—mind, body, heart, sensuality, and spirit.

About Entertainment Psychology

After all the information presented, there has been a petition posted with the American Psychological Association (APA) advocating for the development of a specialized focus called Entertainment Psychology, which will be devoted to the scholarly and practical study of the psychological aspects and unique stressors encountered within the entertainment industry. Similarly, a documentary and/or televised series highlighting and developing constructive dialogue around the shadow aspects of the entertainment industry—with testimonies from entertainers, athletes, psychologists, and other professionals throughout the industry—is an additional aspiration.

Entertainers and athletes are more than what is portrayed in the news and tabloids, on television, and on the big screen. Whether there are pre-existing psychological conditions that are exacerbated by unique stressors or psychological, distress-induced conditions from the unique stressors of the entertainment industry, it is time to advocate for preventative measures as well as health and wellness throughout the industry.

Other Books by Mimi Amaral

Bright Lights, Dark Shadows: An Integrative Literature Review of the Shadow Side of The Psychological Consequences of Celebrity and Fame for Entertainers, 2016, Published by ProQuest LLC

Connect with the Author

Website: mimipsy-d.com

Email: mimi@mimipsy-d.com

Social Media:

Facebook: https://www.facebook.com/
entertainmentpsychology

LinkedIn: https://www.linkedin.com/in/
mimi-psyd-b772a3159

Twitter: @MimiPsyd

Instagram: mimi.psyd

Acknowledgements

First, acknowledgement and gratitude to Source/ Cosmos [AKA: God]. Without divine guidance, none of this would have manifested.

Note: "Always give credit where credit is due. Never allow someone else to take the gratitude, especially when they did not help manifest and only created chaos or made things harder."

~ Mimi

Gratitude to...

My mom: For your encouragement to me to advocate for others.

Dr. T. Gagar: For your encouragement and editing of this book.

Dr. David Schroerlucke: For your encouragement, signing original documentation, and being part of the steering committee for Entertainment Psychology.

Dr. Richard Carolan: For signing the original documentation and being part of the steering committee for Entertainment Psychology.

Dr. Bryant Welch: For signing the original documentation and being part of the steering committee for Entertainment Psychology.

References

Abrams, K., and G. Robinson. "Occupational effects of stalking." *Can J Psychiatry* 47, no. 5 (2002): 468-72.

"Actor Johnathon Schaech: I was Molested By Director Franco Zeffirelli." *People*, January 11, 2018.

"Actors and typecasting." Raindance, Nov. 27, 2012.

Almukhtar, S." After Weinstein: 71 Men Accused Of Sexual Misconduct And Their Fall From Power." *The New York Times*, November 10, 2017.

Aramovitch, Seth. "Corey Feldman on Alijah Wood Hollywood Pedophilia Controversy, 'I Would Love To Name Names.'" *Hollywood Reporter*, May, 25, 2016.

Ballard, G. "The Nightmare on Pill Street!" *The American Chiropractor*, November 25, 2012.

Bangs Show Biz. "Jane Fonda: Ageism In Hollywood Is 'Alive And Well.'" *Washington Post*, May 25, 2015.

Beal, C. "Loneliness in older women: A review of the literature." *Mental Health Nursing*27, no. 7 (2006): 795–813.

Bjerkeset, O., H. Nordahl, S. Larsson, A. Dahl, and O. Linaker. "A 4-year follow-up study of syndromal and sub-syndromal anxiety and depression symptoms in the general population." *Social Psychiatry and Psychiatric Epidemiology*43, no. 3 (2008): 192–199.

BJS. "Indicators Of School Crime And Safety." *Bureau Of Justice Statistics: IES National Center For Education Statistics*, 2013.

Bly, R. *A Little Book on the Human Shadow*. San Francisco, CA: Harper and Row, 1988.

Bonawitz, A. "Tara Reid opens up about plastic surgery." CBS News, October 13, 2006.

Boorstin, D.J. *The Image: A Guide to Pseudo-Events in America*. New York, NY: Random House, 1961.

Bora, C. "Negative effects of plastic surgery." *Buzzle*, March 8, 2012.

Braudy, L. *The Frenzy of Renown Fame and its History*. New York, NY: Vintage Books, 1986.

Bryant, J., and P. Vorderer. *Psychology of Entertainment*. New York, NY: Lawrence Erlbaum, 2006.

"Categories of Stalking." University of New Mexico Judicial Education Center, 2013.

"Celebrity, n.," *OED Online*. 2015, Oxford University Press.

Chia, J., and N. Hensley. "Olympic Gymnast McKayla Maroney Says Team Doctor Repeatedly Molested Her." *New York Daily News*, October 18, 2017.

Chopra, D., D. Ford, and M. Williams. "Unmasking the shadow." In *The Shadow Effect: Illuminating the Hidden Power of Your True Self*, vol. 1, 1-179. New York, NY: Harper One, 2010.

Cicchetti, J. "The role of Jung's concept of shadow in homeopathic treatment." *American Journal of Homeopathic Medicine* 97(2004): 15–20.

Clark, H. "Confessions of a celebrity mom: Brooke Shields's *Down Came the Rain: My Journey Through Postpartum Depression*." *Canadian Review of American Studies* 38, no. 3 (2008): 449–461.

Collins, B. "The funniest man of a generation, dead at 63."*Esquire Magazine*, August 11, 2014.

Corrigan, P., and A. Matthews." Stigma and disclosure: Implications for coming out of the closet." *Journal of Mental Health*12, no. 3 (2003): 235–248.

Cowen, T. "Which athletes and entertainers choose to come out of the closet?" *Marginal Revolution*, May 6, 2013.

Crain, W. "Jung." *Encounter: Education for Meaning and Social Justice* 16, no. 3 (2003): 1–5.

Collins, G. "The family; celebrity families: Problems of success." *The New York Times*, September 23, 1985.

"'Coming out as a gay actor ruined my career in Hollywood,' says actor Rupert Everett." *The Daily Mail*, December 2, 2009.

Cosgrove-Mather, B. "Fighting ageism in Hollywood." CBS News, August 1, 2002.

Curry, C. "Celebrities and heroin addiction: How it happens." ABC News, February 4, 2014.

Curry, R. "The employment contract with the minor under California civil code section 36: Does the 'Coogan Law' adequately protect the minor?" *Journal of Juvenile Law* 7 (1983): 93–98.

Danity. "Ten celebrities who suffer from anxiety/panic disorder." Blog post, December 29, 2011.

De Backer, C.J., M. Nelissen, P. Vyncke, J. Braeckman, and F.T. McAndrew. "Celebrities: from teachers to friends." *Human Nature* 18, no. 4(2007): 334–354.

Dennison, S.M., and D.M. Thomson. "Identifying stalking: the relevance of intent in commonsense reasoning." *Law and Human Behavior* 26, no.5 (2002): 543–561.

Diamond, S. "Essential secrets of psychotherapy: What is the 'shadow'?" *Psychology Today*, April 20, 2012.

Dittmann, M. "Fighting ageism." *American Psychological Association Monitor* 34, no. 5 (2003): 1–50.

Dittmann, M. "Plastic surgery: Beauty or beast?" *American Psychological Association Monitor* 36, no. 8(2005): 1–30.

Eggenberger, N. "Mel Gibson's expletive-ridden rant tape released." *Us Weekly*, April 19, 2012.

Emanuel, S. "The advance of the paparazzi and the celebrity army." *University of Southern California Dissertations and Theses*, 2007.

"Entertainer, n.," *OED Online*. 2015, Oxford University Press.

Estroff-Maranno, H. "The dangers of loneliness." *Psychology Today*, July 1, 2003.

Evans, A., and G.D. Wilson. *Fame: The Psychology of Stardom*. London, England: Satin, 1999.

"Everybody Knew Corey Feldman And Corey Haim Were 'Passed Around' To Hollywood Pedophiles." Fox News, May 26, 2018.

Falk, B. *Robert Downey, Jr.: The Rise and Fall of the Comeback Kid*. London, England: Portico Books, 2010.

Feldman, C. *Coreyography: A Memoir*. New York, NY: Martin's Press, 2013.

Ferris, K., and S. Harris. *Stargazing: Celebrity, Fame, and Social Interaction.* New York, NY: Routledge, 2011.

Fisher, L. "Anxious celebrities: Stars with anxiety." ABC News, October 2, 2012.

Gamson, J. *Claims to Fame Celebrity in Contemporary America.* Berkeley, CA: University of California Press, 1994.

"Garth Brooks takes Chris Gaines on media rounds." CNN News, September 30, 1999.

Gates, B. *Privacy Quotes,* 2001.

Gauthier, R. "New law hits aggressive paparazzi." *Los Angeles Times,* December 30, 2005.

Giles, D. *Illusions of Immortality: A Psychology of Fame and Celebrity.* New York, NY: St. Martin's Press, 2010.

Goldstein, T. "Psychological perspectives on acting." *Psychology of Aesthetics 3,* no. 1 (2009): 6–9.

Grann, K. "To die for—Robert Blake, Bonnie Lee Bakley and the misery of celebrity." *The New Republic,* April 13, 2001.

Gray, M. "Despite age discrimination there is still beauty in the world." *The Huffington Post,* June 7, 2010.

Gross, D. "Twitter reviews policies after Robin Williams' daughter harassed." CNN News, August 14, 2014.

Hall-Flavin, D. "What does it mean to have a nervous breakdown?" *Mayo Clinic*, January 31, 2014.

Halpern, J. *Fame Junkies: The Hidden Truths Behind America's Favorite Addiction*. New York, NY: Houghton Mifflin Company, 2007.

Harbin, C. *Carl Jung's concept of the shadow: Applying psychology to real life situations*. October 20, 2006.

Harvey, D. *Obsession: Celebrities and Their Stalkers*. Dublin, Ireland: Merlin, 2002.

Hilden, J. "Does celebrity destroy privacy: Naomi Campbell and narcotics anonymous." *FindLaw News*, April 2, 2002.

"Hollywood? It's Finished, Claims Oscar-Winning Director Who Fled To New York." *The Guardian*, October 21, 2017.

Horowitz, A. "Robin Williams dead: Beloved actor dies in apparent suicide." *The Huffington Post*, August 11, 2014.

Houston, R. "Weekend Miley Cyrus news: Robin Thicke split, mocks engagement, new lesbian kiss." *Examiner*, March 1, 2014.

Howe, P. *Paparazzi: And Our Obsession with Celebrity*. New York, NY: Workman, 2005.

Howell, C. "Darius Rucker: If it's not a country song, I don't want to play it." *Taste of Country*, April 19, 2014.

Johnson, R. *Owning Your Own Shadow: Understanding the Dark Side of the Psyche.* New York, NY: Harper One, 1991.

Kaufman, G. "Lindsay Lohan car-crash photographer not charged." MTV News, December 29, 2005.

Kelley, S. "Heather Graham Takes On Sexism In Film And Relationships With Her Directorial Debut 'Half Magic.'" *LA Times*, February, 27, 2018.

Kiwi, . *True Michael Jackson: in his own words and in words of those who knew him.* January 1, 2012

Kluwer, W. "Drug related deaths—Notable celebrities."*Drugs.com*, May 4, 2014.

Langcaster-James, H. "Fame may lead to a shorter life." BBC News, April 17, 2013.

Lawrence, C. *Cult of Celebrity: What Our Fascination with the Stars Reveals About Us*. Guilford, CT: Globe Pequot, 2009.

Leicht, L., and S. Colino. "Forty-three inspiring celebrities who lived with depression." *The Huffington Post*, October 31, 2011.

Libow, J.A. "Traumatized children and the news media: Clinical considerations." *American Journal of Orthopsychiatry*62, no. 3 (1992): 379–386.

"Lindsay Lohan experiences rehab meltdown, and is completely lifeless without Adderall." *Inquisitr*, May 21, 2013.

Lovett, K. "Utah Victims Say NY Kid Abuse Laws Are Too Weak, Join Fight To Enact Child Victim Act." *New York Daily News*, February 27, 2018.

Lovett, K. "Actor Corey Feldman Confronts NY Senators Opposed To Passage Of The Child Victims Act At State Capitol." *New York Daily News*, March 14, 2018.

Lutz, A. "Seventeen celebrity before-and-after plastic surgery disasters." *Business Insider*, August 7, 2012.

MacNab, G. "Homophobia in Hollywood: Why gay movie stars still can't come out of the closet." *The Independent*, January 18, 2013.

Maltby, J., J. Houran, and L. McCutcheon. "A clinical interpretation of attitudes and behaviors associated with celebrity worship." *Nervous and Mental Disease* 191 (2003): 25–29.

Maninno, B. "Ten worst celebrity plastic surgery mishaps." *Woman's Day*, May 18, 2013.

McCutcheon, L., R. Lange,and J. Houran. "Conceptualization and measurement of celebrity worship." *British Journal of Psychology* 93 (2002): 67–87.

McCutcheon, L., M. Aruguete, V.B. Scott, and K.L. VonWaldner. "Preference for solitude and attitude toward one's favorite celebrity." *North American Journal of Psychology* 6, no. 3 (2004): 499–506.

McCutcheon, L., D. Ashe, J. Houran, and J. Maltby. "A cognitive profile of individuals who tend to worship celebrities." *Journal of Psychology* 137, no. 4 (2003): 309-322.

McCutcheon, L., V. Scott., M. Aruguete, and J. Parker. "Exploring the link between attachment and the inclination to obsess about or stalk celebrities." *North American Journal of Psychology* 8, no. 2(2006):289–300.

McCutcheon, L., M. Aruguete, V.B. Scott, J.S. Parker, and J.J. Calicchia. "The development and validation of an indirect measure of celebrity stalking." *North American Journal of Psychology* 8, no.3 (2006): 503–516.

McKay, H. "Golden Globes: Jodie Foster hints at being gay, retirement in strange 'lonely' speech." Fox News, January 14, 2013.

Mentel, T. "Seven actors who always play the same characters." *The Entertainment Cheat Sheet*, December 17, 2013.

"Michael Jackson admits his feeling of loneliness." MTV News, May 8, 2014.

Moloney, Aisling. "What Is A Casting Couch And What Cases Are There From Hollywood?" *Metro News*, October 12, 2017.

Muller, R. "In the limelight: Celebrities struggling with mental health." *Psychology Today*, July 26, 2013.

Murray, R. "Keeping the paparazzi an arm's length away." *The Journal of Popular Culture*46, no. 4 (2013): 868–885.

Neimark, J. "The culture of celebrity." *Psychology Today*, May 1, 1995.

Neuman, F. "Determining suicide risk part 1: Suicide 'gestures,' suicide attempts, and suicide." *Psychology Today*, August 6, 2012.

Nichols, J. "Raven Symone fans tweet 'childhood ruined' after star comes out." *The Huffington Post*, August 8, 2013.

Nord, W.R., and J.M. Jermier. "Overcoming resistance to resistance: insights from a study of the shadows." *Public Administration Quarterly* 17, no. 4(1994): 396-409.

Novarro, M. "I love you with all my hype." *The New York Times*, May 22, 2005.

O'Neal, T. *A Paper Life*. New York, NY: Harper Collins, 2004.

OWN. "Alanis Morissette on the trauma of fame: I didn't laugh for 2 years (video)." *Huffington Post*, September 18,2014.

Parker, A. "Corey Feldman Announces Project to Expose Hollywood Pedophilia." CBS News, October 25, 2017.

Park, M. "Keven Spacey Apologizes For Alleged Sex Assault With A Minor." CNN, October, 31, 2017.

Peeples, J. "Meredith Baxter on ageism and Hollywood's effect on homophobia." *Advocate*, July 8, 2014.

Penetrante, N. "A beautiful life: Understanding Carl Jung's archetype of shadow." March 15, 2012.

Pfeiffer, B., F. Kardes, and S. Posavac. "The less the public knows the better? The effects of increased knowledge on celebrity evaluations." *Basic and Applied Social Psychology* 34, no. 6 (2012): 499-507.

Pisani, L. "Why would anyone want to date Sean Penn?" *The New York Post*, March 14, 2015.

Phillips, M. *High on Arrival: A Memoir*. New York, NY: Gallery Books, 2009.

Pomerantz, D. "Why Ellen Page coming out matters." *Forbes*, February 16, 2014.

Presley, E. *Quotes about Celebrity.* 2014.

Quinn, B. "The Bureau of Justice Statistics: Stalking." September 1, 2012.

Raeburn, S. D. "Occupational stress and coping in a sample of professional rock musicians." *Medical Problems of Performing Artists*2, no. 2 (1987): 41–48.

Raeburn, S. D. "The Ring of Fire: Shame, Fame, and Rock 'n' Roll." *Medical Problems of Performing Artists*22, no. 1 (2007): 3–9.

Rahman, M. "Jane O'Connor, the cultural significance of the child star." *Canadian Journal of Sociology* 33, no. 3 (2008): 752–754.

Rapport, L., and M. Meleen. "Childhood celebrity, parental attachment, and adult adjustment: The young performers study." *Journal of Personality Assessment* 70, no. 3(1998): 484-505.

Richo, D. *Shadow Dance: Liberating the Power and Creativity of Your Dark Side.* Boston, MA: Shambhala, 1999.

Robb, B. J. *Heath Ledger: Hollywood's Dark Star.* London, England: Plexus, 2008.

Rockwell, D., and D.C. Giles. "Being a celebrity: A phenomenology of fame." *Journal of Phenomenological Psychology* 40(2009):179–210.

Rockwell, D., and D.C. Giles. "Celebrity and being-in-the-world: The experience of being famous." Presented at the annual meeting of the International Communication Association. New York, NY, 2004.

Sager, J. "Corey Feldman: Corey Haim And I Were 'Passed Around' to Hollywood Pedophiles." *New York Post*, May 26, 2016.

Sauerwein, S. *Celebrity Stalkers: The Unfortunate Price of Fame.* Calgary, Alberta, Canada: Altitude, 2006.

Sentrypc. "Are Your Children Protected." 2018.

Serafino, J. "The 10 most typecast actors." *Complex*, October 26, 2012.

Singh, A. "Scarlett Johansson: Women actresses are victims of Hollywood ageism." *The Telegraph*, August 12, 2008.

Smalley, B., and W. McIntosh. "The loss of fame: Psychological implications." *The Journal of Popular Culture* 44, no. 2 (2011): 385–397.

Stevens, M. "Britney Spears, outsider artist." *New York Magazine*, October 24, 2007.

Stever, G. S. "Fan behavior and lifespan development theory: Explaining para-social and social attachment to celebrities." *Journal of Adult Development* 18, no. 1 (2011): 1-7.

Stever, G. S., and K. Lawson. "Twitter as a way for celebrities to communicate with fans: Implications for the study of parasocial interaction." *North American Journal of Psychology* 15, no. 2 (2013): 339–354.

Swami, V., T. Chamorro-Premuzic, K. Mastor, F. Siran, M. Said, J. Jaafar, and S.K. Pillai. "Celebrity worship among university students in Malaysia: A methodological contribution to the celebrity attitude scale." *European Psychologist* 16, no. 4(2011): 334–342.

Sykes, T. "Alijah Wood Calls Out Hollywood's Pedophilia." *Daily Beast*, May 23, 2016.

Syrmopoulos, J. "Hollywood Crumbles As Hollywood Oscar-Winning Director Suggests Cover-Up Of Wide Spread Pedophilia." The Free Thought Project, October 24, 2017.

Tatliliouglu, K. "The effect of cognitive behavioral oriented psycho education program on dealing with loneliness: An online psychological counseling approach." *Education* 134, no. 1 (2013): 101–109.

Tauber, M. "A life cut short: Corey Monteith: 1982-2013."*People* 80, no. 5 (2013):49-53.

Torraco, R. J. "Writing integrative literature reviews: Guidelines and examples." *Human Resource Development Review* 4, no. 3 (2005): 356–367.

Trent, T. "Expired: Ageism, sexism and women in the music industry." *Trini Trent,* August 2, 2013.

Turner, G. *Understanding Celebrity.* Thousand Oaks, CA: Sage, 2004.

Turner, G. "Approaching celebrity studies." *Celebrity Studies* 1, no. 1 (2010): 11-20.

"Two proposed divisions address our changing world." *American Psychological Association,* November 22, 2012.

Vagianos, Alanna. "140 Women Have Accused Larry Nassar Of Abuse. His Victims Think We Don't Care." *Huffington Post,* January 14, 2018.

Van Dijk, W.W., J.W. Ouwerkerk, G.M. van Koningsbruggen, and Y.M. Wesseling. "So you wanna be a pop star?: Schadenfreude following another's misfortune on TV." *Basic and Applied Social Psychology* 34, no.2 (2012): 168–174.

Watercutter, A. "Tina Fey Nailed It: Hollywood Has A Serious Ageism Problem." *Wired,* February 17, 2017.

Watt, K. "Top 10 self-destructive child actors." October 2008.

Young, S.M. "Report: Former NFL Lineman Jonathan Martin Checks Into Mental Health Facility." *Sports Yahoo,* February 26, 2018.

Zengerle, J. "Not since Jesus." *NewYork Magazine,* 2006.

Zweig, C. "Tracing the roots of the shadow in culture." In *Romancing the Shadow: A Guide to Soul Work for a Vital, Authentic Life,* edited by C. Zweig and S. Wolf, 52–55. New York, NY: Ballantine, 1997.

Zweig, C., and J. Abrams. *Meeting the Shadow: The Hidden Power of the Dark Side of Human Nature.* New York, NY: G.P. Putnam's Sons, 1990.

www.ingramcontent.com/pod-product-compliance
Lightning Source LLC
Chambersburg PA
CBHW070809290326
41931CB00011BB/2178